ADMINISTRATIVE RESPONSIVENESS IN INDIA

Perceptions, Analysis and Model Building

ADMINISTRATIVE RESPONSIVENESS IN INDIA

Perceptions, Analysis and Model Building

Pardeep Sahni
and
E. Vayunandan

MANOHAR
1992

ISBN: 81-7304-008-7

First Published 1992

Published by
Ajay Kumar Jain
Manohar Publishers & Distributors
2/6, Ansari Road, Daryaganj,
New Delhi - 110002

Lasertypeset by
A J Software Publishing Co. Pvt. Ltd.
305 Durga Chambers,
Karol Bagh
New Delhi- 110005

Printed at
Elegant Printers
A-38/2 Maya Puri Phase-I
New Delhi-110 064

Preface

Public administration as a discipline is a specialised body of knowledge. There may be differences in regard to the specifics of the knowledge and its scope and boundaries but there is substantial unanimity with regard to the study of its various components, viz., politico-legal institutions and their processes; economic and social institutions and their processes; concepts of organisation and administration; financial administration concepts, tools and techniques; and techniques of analysis.

Public administration, in the words of Fredrick Mosher, "is a reasonably clear-cut occupational field which offers a lifetime career to its members". Besides being a reasonably defined occupational field and specialised body of knowledge, public administration is an ideal of service and indicator of proper conduct and functionalism in the field. As a system it could be likened to the skeletal system in a human body which cannot function without the former.

The dependence on the government is increasing every day. The governmental administrative system has proliferated in innumberable areas. Commenting upon the issue "What's gone wrong with Public Administration", Peter Self poses a question. Has Public Administration become overloaded with excessive responsibilities and expectations? According to him, overloading of Public Administration refers to the increased expectations which have further led to a substantive increase in formal tasks and responsibilities of the government.

A number of issues stem out of the point made by Peter Self: Why has the governmental administration taken so much upon it? Has the increase been forced on it by the political system? Is it because the private entrepreneurs do not wish to enter into the concerned areas? Is it that the administrative organisations do not want to part with authority because of their own interests? Is the governmental administration doing justice to its responsibilities? What support and cooperation is the administration getting from political parties, pressure groups, voluntary organisations, and citizens for performing its tasks? And, is the administration keen to create supplemental channels or seek support and cooperation from the rest?

From whichever angle one may look at, one thing stands out -- that the citizens are not getting appropriate response from the administration. Who is to be held responsible for this -- administration, political executive, legislature, judiciary, voluntary organisations, pressure groups, citizens, or all of them? What is idealistically as well as pragmatically required is a system of administration which not only owns its responsibility but also shows concern for general welfare through its actions.

What does administrative responsiveness mean? By which techniques Public Administration, particularly at the lower levels -- in India could be made more responsible, responsive and accountable? These are some of the aspects which have been analyzed in the present work. Keeping in view the fact that several studies at different levels have already been conducted which, by and large, reveal the level and degree of the administration's response to the citizens and the system, we did not make this study data based. Instead, we have garnered the views and perceptions of some of the distinguished political leaders and administrators.

All those personalities despite their very busy schedule were generous with their time and provided us an opportunity of recording their scholarly, philosophical and meaningful impressions and feelings. For this we owe a deep sense of gratitude to Shri Arun Bhagat, IPS, Commissioner, Delhi Police; Shri B.B Vohra, IAS (Retd.); formerly Secretary to Government of India, Ministry of Petroleum; Professor G. Ram Reddy, Chairman, University Grants Commission; Shri H.D. Shourie, IAS (Retd.), Director, Ministry of Urban Development, Government of India; Shri Harkishan Singh Surjeet, General Secretary, Communist Party of India (Marxist); Shri Indrajit Gupta, MP, General Secretary, Communist Party of India; Shri K.C.Pant, formerly Union Defence Minister; Shri L.K.Advani, MP, Leader of the opposition in Lok Sabha; Shri R.D. Kitson, Chairman, Railway Board; Shri Ram Jethmalani, MP, eminent jurist; Professor Subramaniam Swamy, MP, formerly Union Commerce Minister; Shri T.N. Chaturvedi, IAS (Retd), formerly Comptroller and Auditor General of India; Professor V.C.Kulandai Swamy, Vice-Chancellor, Indira Gandhi National Open University; Raja Vijay Karan, IPS, Director, Central Bureau of Investigation; and Shri Yashwant Sinha, MP, formerly Union Finance Minister. An analysis of the mature views of these dignitaries provides useful directions for making the administration responsive. Besides, informal discussions were held with a number of political leaders, administrators, technocrats, and academics for adding qualitative inputs.

We feel beholden to Professor S.P. Verma, Professor D.R. Sachdeva, Professor Pandav Nayak, Professor Kapil Kumar, Ms. Alka Dhemaja, Ms. Uma Medury, Ms. Indira Mukerjee and Dr. Debal K. Singha Roy for their useful suggestions. We would be failing in our duty if we do not record our gratitude to Shri K.K. Bajaj, presently Chief Engineer with a public sector undertaking, for recounting to us his experiences regarding various facets of the problem discussed in the book.

We gratefully recognize that this effort has been stimulated by the positive sets of values for education held by our parents late Shri S.P. Sahni and Shrimati Raj Rani Sahni.

Special thanks go to Upasana and Vijaya Lakshmi, our wives, for the co-operation and help they gladly extended to us for the completion of this work.

Last but not least, it is Shri Ajay Jain, of Manohar Publishers & Distributors who has taken pains to bring out the book expeditiously.

PARDEEP SAHNI
E. VAYUNANDAN

List of Interviewees*

1. Shri Arun Bhagat, IPS, Commissioner, Delhi Police, New Delhi.
2. Shri B.B. Vohra, IAS (Retd.), Formerly Secretary to Government of India, Ministry of Petroleum, New Delhi.
3. Professor G. Ram Reddy, Chairman, University Grants Commission, New Delhi.
4. Shri H.D. Shourie IAS (Retd.), Director, Common Cause (Voluntary Organisation), New Delhi.
5. Shri Harkishan Singh Surjeet, General Secretary, Communist Party of India (Marxist); New Delhi.
6. Dr. H.S. Anand, IAS, Director, Ministry of Urban Development, Government of India, New Delhi.
7. Shri Indrajit Gupta, Member Parliament, General Secretary Communist Party of India, New Delhi.
8. Shri. K. C. Pant (Congress-I) Formerly Union Defence Minister, New Delhi.
9. Shri. L.K. Advani (Bhartiya Janata Party) Member Parliament, Leader of the Opposition in Lok Sabha, New Delhi.
10. Shri. R.D. Kitson, Chairman, Railway Board, New Delhi.
11. Shri Ram Jethmalani (Janata Dal), Member Parliament, Eminent Jurist, New Delhi.
12. Professor Subramaniam Swamy (Janata Party), Member Parliament, Formerly Union Commerce Minister, New Delhi.
13. Shri T.N. Chaturvedi, IAS (Retd.), Formerly Comptroller and Auditor General of India, New Delhi.
14. Professor V.C. Kulandai Swamy, Vice-Chancellor, Indira Gandhi National Open University, New Delhi.
15. Shri Vijay Karan, IPS, Director, Central Bureau of Investigation, New Delhi.
16. Shri Yashwant Sinha, IAS (Retd)., (Samajwadi Janata Party), Member Parliament, Foremerly Union Finance Minister, New Delhi.

---

* Positions/Designations shown are as they existed at the time interviews were conducted.

1

Need of the Day

The importance and significance of Public Administration is steadily growing with the ongoing expansion of state operations in the present age. Irrespective of the type of polity, one finds universalistic expansion in the role of Public Administration. Whenever there have been efforts to transform a traditional society into a modern one, there have been clearly defined goals to accomplish it in a properly defined and spelt out manner. Such modernisation of the state and society has made the State take up the new role of accelerating economic and social change. It also has on its active performance agenda the major responsibility of providing the required standards of life, health, education, clean environment, and both qualitative and quantitative opportunities of employment and care of the aged group of its citizens. Enormous stress on developmental activities, rise of industrialisation, growth of urbanisation, emphasis on functional specialisation, welfare philosophy of the State, etc., are some of the important factors leading to a substantial expansion of state's functions. All these reasons combined together have led to the governing system becoming over-loaded with excessive responsibilities and expectations.

It goes without saying that in any type of polity the major task of the governing/administrative bodies is to work for its citizens in a manner whereby they could get the maximum benefit. In a democratic system, the government is not only of and by the people but also for them. The bureaucracy or the administration has quite a substantial role to play in the overall functioning of a system. It is the administration, as it is often believed, which could improve or harm the set-up under its charge and make the citizens satisfied or dissatisfied with the system through the working of the administration. It is a fact that through administration the clientele group in the form of citizens could seek benefits, justice and whatever is due to them at an appropriate time without any delays and harassment. The citizens depend a lot on the administration because it is this agency which is responsible for translating into action the policies and programmes formulated by the political representatives of the citizens. Right from birth till death the citizens come not only in quantitative but also in qualitative contact with the administration. At every point in life, whether walking on road, residing in home, studying in an educational institution, working in an organisation, seeking retirement or superannuation benefits, getting medical care in hospitals, the citizens find no alternative other than to depend and look towards the administration as it is through it that the various policies of the governmment affecting each and every aspect of life are being put to execution. Right from the basic and elementary needs to the luxurious necessities they have to get the things move and done by those who are administering the affairs. It is through the aid, assistance and help of the administration that the citizens enjoy political, civic and economic rights, use civic amenities as well as public utilities and keenly look forward to a meaningful exploitation of the possible resources in an optimum manner for their ultimate benefit.

During the past few decades, even the underdeveloped or developing nations have seen significant transformation in numerous aspects of their lives with tremendous social progress, unprecedented geographic mobility and tremendous traditional hierarchies. All these factors have created a progressive awareness among a sizeable number of citizens. Because of this increase in awareness a feeling has developed amongst them that their genuine concerns should be dealt with responsibly, promptly, and effectively by the administration, because it is the administration which, in a majority of the cases, is at a giving or deciding point. What is thus expected of the administration is that it should not be lethargic, whimsical and should not interpret the rules and regulations negatively.

It is normally a point of belief and an expectation of the citizens that the administration should be responsive to the needs of the public at large. What is administrative responsiveness? Is it virtually the role-plank of the administration to be responsive?, and could it be responsive, as expected and aspired for by the citizens and the system without the active support of the other related and much important agencies/institutions?, are some of the significant questions which need to be addressed.

Administrative Responsiveness

The meaning of the word 'Responsive' is to make one reply to; answer to; correspond to; and be suitable to the issues at hand. Thus, the term 'administrative responsiveness' means responding to, reflecting and giving expression to the will of the people. A few things emerge out of the explanation of the word 'responsive' and the term 'administrative responsiveness' given above. Replying to, answering to, corresponding to, etc. which reveal the meaning of the word 'responsive' show that these are subjective aspects. The administrator 'A' may respond to or correspond to the case, grievance, or enquiry made by citizen 'X' in a manner based upon his own logic and perception of the issue or situation. It may be altogether a different interpretation having been made of the same issue by another administrator 'B'. Likewise, responding to or giving expression to the will of the people, as stated above brings to light the values involved in the will. The will of a citizen or group of citizens may have been fashioned by him or them to be translated into favourable decision by the administration suiting the personal interest of the concerned citizen or group of citizens. Certainly, this becomes a debatable point in itself. But what is required of the administration's responsiveness or through administrative responsiveness is to address to the grievances of the people clarifying the government's orders, instructions and policies and educating the public about these issues at length. With passage of time the citizens' faith in an administration is on the negative side and they develop a feeling that public comforts and conveniences are not properly considered by the administration, applications, requests, and grievances are not disposed off speedily, effectively and judiciously, and nothing gets done in a government organisation without resorting to either corruption or using the influence of political masters or the top administration for getting even the most genuine cases decided.

Government, more so of a welfare state, is responsible for socio-economic development and uplift of the people, besides maintaining routine law and order. One of the Directive Principles of the State Policy says: "the State shall strive to promote the welfare of the people by securing and protecting as effectively as it may, a social order in which justice, social, economic and political, shall inform all institutions of the national life. The State shall in particular strive to minimise the inequalities in income and endeavour to eliminate inequalities in facilities and opportunities not only amongst individuals but also amongst groups of people residing in different areas or engaged in different vocations''. These words from the Constitution clearly make it the responsibility of the Governmental machinery to provide a type of administration which is of optimum utility and interest to the community at large. Leaving aside the scope of negativities which could emerge because of the subjectivity and values involved in the overall meaning of the administrative responsiveness, this term means such actions on the part of administration as not only serve but also appear to have served the interests of the people in a just, fair and impartial manner. The administration should be capacitated to maintain constitutional order; achieve technical and professional competence and above all behave ethically. All this is required to cope with public expectations; come up to their increased aspirations; and to contribute towards the overall development and growth of the country in the interest of the masses.

Administrative responsiveness implies people-oriented administration. Government programmes have not only grown but have expanded manifold and changed their form and with it have expanded bureaucratic responsibilities and obligations, its commitment to the tasks, and expectations of the citizens for the performance of the same by it in efficient and effective ways. It won't be wrong to say that a feature of most structural adjustment plans is a requirement for greater efficiency in administration aiming at committed responsiveness to the needs of the citizens at lower costs.

Administrative responsiveness implies that in government the administrative machinery at the contact point has to be strong and responsive enough not only for delivering the goods to the citizens effectively but also to act to the satisfaction of all concerned. To this end, the tasks of administration include: appropriate constitutional provisions for ensuring timely and regular elections to local institutions; decentralised district planning alongwith constitutional provisions spelling out the subjects in the district sector; restructuring of personnel policies and training programmes in the light of the growing interface between the administration and political bodies on the one hand and administration and citizens on the other; innovations and flexibility in office procedures and programme administration at the implementation level; clear definition of tasks and accountability of government functionaries; timely and speedy redressal of public grievances; and improvement in working environment, etc.

1.2 Administrative Responsiveness: Need and Significance

The administration is the vehicle of development and its role becomes crucial in developing or underdeveloped nations more so because, firstly, the citizens do not have healthy precedents and broader mental horizons to think beyond their parochial interests and secondly, much is required to be attained on developmental fronts. In addition, political bodies are not strong enough to offer a really helping hand to the administration in its efforts to come up to the expectations of the people in particular and society in general.

In an independent, democratic, and welfare state, the citizens occupy quite an important position. They are the ones who are not only being governed but also govern by way of exercising their right of franchise and electing their representatives who in turn formulate policies in accordance with which the administrators are supposed to govern for the benefit of the society. The benefits are to be accorded to or conferred on the citizens by the administration in a manner whereby absolute optimality is attained and no one is favoured or deprived of at the cost of or for favouring some one. In such a system, it is expected of the administration to provide to all the members of the society a standard of life which is satisfactory and without any risks of insecurity or stagnation on the economic front. In a nutshell, what is required is the complete and overall development of an individual's personality without having any fear of suspicion and mistrust towards the system in his mind. By and large the citizens in developing nations are keen and anxious to receive the benefits without caring for rules, procedures, and mechanisms evolved for that purpose. They always feel that they are at the receiving end and have no positive contribution to make as things happen in accordance with the rules framed for the purpose. This feeling becomes more strong when even on one or two occasions they find the administration behaving in an arbitrary or zany ways. Taking the example of India, one could say that since independence there has been tremendous socio-economic development. It is one of the most advanced countries in the third world having its own highly developed atomic power projects. It is the seventh most industrialised nation in the world having the third largest pool of engineers, doctors and technocrats and stands fourth in agricultural production. Making a comparison of this development with the development in the thinking of the people of India, there is still a vast gap. "The transformation has not taken place in the mental attitudes in our country, in the minds of our people — to a large extent, we still remain prisoners of concepts, concepts that were evolved at an earlier time, concepts that were designed to face a different set of challenges in different circumstances with different opportunities and where a different set of options was available. These concepts have served us very well during these forty years. But it is essential now to look at them afresh. There is no excuse to absolve us of the responsibility of giving things a fresh look."[1] As a result of still not having been out of mental depresssion and bankruptcy of developmental ideals and attitudes, it becomes all the more essential for the administration to be more productive, strong and respond quickly to the demands and needs of the people not only for building in them confidence but also for ensuring their cooperation for ushering in more developmental tasks.

Administrative responsiveness is required for looking at the opportunities for bringing up not only more developmental activities but also for attempting to establish healthy linkages with the programmes having been executed at the grassroots and the international agencies. The administration cannot, in such a scenario, afford to remain bogged down only with the philosophical outlook or bent of mind of its citizens. The administration has to be capacitated in itself not to isolate the developmental affairs at grassroot level from the bearing of foreign policies or international affairs of the nation. The administration's responsiveness is a must for not looking at such policies and programmes from their linkages between the contact point and international levels in different boxes.

Keeping in vicw thc vicwpoint of the citizens, their mental attitudes, the developmental tasks and the linkages between those at the grassroots and national and international levels, the administrative responsiveness does mean that the administration must try to completely understand the past culture and traditions in order to spell out clearly its mode of operation for the present as well as the future. Whatever is found as useful and worth its salt in the past culture, traditions, and habits must be attempted to be cherished and made use of for building up the administrative strategies for the future. Administrative responsiveness could not be made effective unless either the long inherited values are used or the ones which have outlived their utility are done away with by making the constituents of the society convinced of the same.

There is need for administrative responsiveness also for making the administration and all the persons involved in it think and put to practice the ideas, schemes and innovations pertaining to their specified role and operational jurisdiction in a much more broad and integrative sense. For example, the schemes in agriculture cannot be made effective unless the administrator in the agricultural sector tries to look upon those in accordance with the related irrigation, electricity, and fertilizer sectors. Development certainly does not come through by attempting it in parts. Therefore, an integrative whole has to be kept in view.

Men, material and finances are the three important resources for bringing in development and modernisation. A thorough probe into the utility and significance of these three resources brings to light that the manpower outnumbers the remaining two for the assigned purposes. The best of the machines and the finances are to be managed, operated, generated and accounted for by men. Moreover, human beings possess the brains to think. Administration needs to be alert and effective to properly make use of the most important resource on the earth, that is, the human being, by performing its tasks, duties and obligations in an efficient, responsible and effective manner. Human beings if properly tapped could do wonders for making any system a great success. Simultaneously, it should not be forgotten that if human beings develop a negative picture of any system they could not only mar its growth but could also be held responsible for completely turning things upside down.

Every system has some tangible goals to attain or strive for. For example, the larger goals of the Indian system are democracy, secularism, socialism and development of humanity. The administration could get maximum cooperation from the elected bodies of the people at all levels and more so at the cutting edges of the administration. The reason for it is that the elected representatives of the people are there in such bodies and are aware of the needs and compulsions of their electorate as well as areas. Instead of getting afraid of the politically elected bodies, the administration needs to strengthen the elected bodies at the grassroots in order to solicit the support and cooperation of such bodies for making the administration more strong and active. Unfortunately, the situation in India with regard to local elected bodies has not been that bright. The concern of the administration being reflected as responsive could be made amply apparent in case the administration attempts to not only get these bodies in existence but also concretise its efforts in getting the maximum out of these for making the working of the administration more to the point. Could an administration be termed as responsive if the minority of the downtrodden in any area of operation are being suppressed. The responsiveness on the part of the administration is to make effective use of constitutional safeguards against social prejudice and economic discrimination.

Consequent upon the processes of economic development in India, the meaning of the word 'Secularism' has become more complex. "The change, the mobility that this is bringing about is engendering group rivalries. The processes of social change are causing uprooting of communities, the disruption of the set system, perhaps even an alienation of certain groups...what is needed is the golden mean between the pursuit of national progress and continuity through traditional values, the golden mean of truth and non-violence, tolerance and compassion, of one humanity and one family of nations."[2] Responsiveness of administration is needed to deal with the related issues of secularism as a law and order issue and the response to communal menace. The administrative responsiveness could be seen if such issues are dealt with by making people abandon their parochial attitudes and looking at things in a bigger and broader perspective of fellowship and fraternity.

Indian socialism is based on the ethical perception that all human beings are part and parcel of a single family and all have to keep track with the basic philosophy that the needs of all are met with in an honourable way. In the light of it, the administration has to make itself responsive and responsible so that the interests of all irrespective of the caste, language, area, sex, education, etc., are protected.

Administration in the present times is facing a number of challenges and pressures which have put its adaptability and capacity to perform to a real and severe test. Efforts have to be made to make the administration energetic and receptive by making itself ready with possible solutions to meet the unknown. Overpopulation, unemployment, widening gap between rich and poor, increase in poverty, rapid industrialisation, craving for more education, technological growth, absolutely mechanistic ways to deal with the problems, etc. are some of the important challenges being faced by the administration. Besides, communal tensions and terrorist activities are also taking considerable time of the administration to deal with the same.

Administrative responsiveness is a must to enable the administration to decentralise, democratise, and humanise itself so that it can keep pace with the quantum of tasks before it. Further, by making it responsive, the administration will be in a position to accept new ideals and make others accept the same thus leading to the ushering in of a new work outlook in its functioning for the challenges ahead.

With the acceleration of social, economic and political changes, the administration needs to be significantly responsive. There is need for the administrators to prepare themselves to anticipate social, economic and political changes and also to capitalise on them. The administrative responsiveness from a point to point in between having a transitory phase has been summed up by Fredrickson[3]. A summary

Table -1

From	Transition	To
The problem is basically one of reform or change (putting right that which is wrong)	Change and reorganization should be encouraged	The problem is one of institutionalizing change procedures (recognising that those things put right are unlikely to stay right and making orrectability criteria as important as correctness)
Rapid social change is a transient phenomenon needing to be weatherd and adjusted to	Organization must attempt to respond to rapid social change	Rapid social change is a permanent phenomenon needing to be facilitated and capitalised upon
The problems occasioned by uncertainity, complexity and rapidity of change require larger investments in organizational machinery increments and development	The problems occasioned by uncertainty, complexity and rapidity of change require modifying already established machinery	The problems occasioned by uncertainty, complexity and rapidity of change require larger investments in decrements and devolution

"Responsiveness" requires effective scanning of open information within the organisation so that it can sense when adaption is required	"Responsiveness" requires widespread participation by clients for purposes of cooptation	"Responsiveness" requires effective scanning of clients and constitiuents so that they can elicit adaption when it is required
Leadership by authority	Leadership by consent	Leadership by change facilitation
Technology may provide the solution to politically "caused" problems	Politics must accommodate technological solutions	Politics may provides solution to technologically "caused" problems

is given in Table-1.

The analysis of the different dimensions of the societal and systems' facets shows that administrative responsiveness is a multi-pronged strategy for coping with not only the present scenario but also to take stock of the anticipated changes in advance and to accordingly prepare the system to perform to the maximum satisfaction of the majority of the constituents. The overall traditions, culture and values existing in the system have to be adhered to and effort made to bring in changes in the outmoded traditions, culture and values through a slow but meaningful transformation. Slow and gradual transformation is required to prepare people to accept the futility of the existing modes and to shift to the new ideals proposed to be ushered in. Efforts ought to be made for making administrative responsiveness in existence, by the agencies involved to not only suggest and bring the changes but also to institutionalise the changes so that it lasts for a longer period and the best out of the same is attained.

The focus of discussion in the preceding analysis on the meaning, need and significance of administrative responsiveness has mainly been on the administration. Of course, besides administration there are other important forces which could contribute to making the administration responsive. The same would be dealt with after examining the meaning of administrative responsibility and accountability and its relationship with administrative responsiveness.

Administrative Responsiveness, Responsibility and Accountability

The meaning, need and significance of administrative responsiveness have been explained in earlier parts. Now firstly, the meaning and significance of administrative responsibility and accountability will be discussed to make out its relationship with administrative responsiveness.

Administrative Responsibility

Politics and administration are not two mutually exclusive boxes. This implies that the administrators have the obligation to not only perform their assigned duties in a competent manner but also in a responsible manner.[4] It is believed that in order to avoid the misuse of power, the same must be accompanied by responsibility. In order to make administrators perform their duties properly it is a must that they are made responsible to the appropriate authorities. It is generally acclaimed that only persons with high sounding morals may be responsible. Strong and stable virtues of character are being indicated through morals. A person who is not stable and normal gets governed not by reasoning but by impulses, not by healthy aptitude but by emotion and such a person does not have any morals. The prerequisites for being responsible are good in case a person is capacitated to develop a stable consistent personality.[5] In the words of Chester I. Barnard "The point is that responsibility is the property of an individual by which whatever morality exists in him becomes effective in conduct". Public administration's attempts to develop an account of such administration which is morally responsible is in existence for the last five decades or so. Though the efforts have been worthwhile, the results have not been very satisfactory. To make a one line answer of the term administrative responsibility would be that it means the proper use of power and authority vested in the administration failing which the incumbent assigned with the job would be held responsible for the same and would be punished or some action taken against him. Administrative responsibility is ensured through various forms of control over administration, viz. control of the legislature, the electorate, the administrative superiors, professional agencies, and the courts.

It was Carl J. Friedrich, who was one of the first to clearly bring forth the problem of administrative responsiveness in the context of a diverse and often divided nation. Administrative responsiveness cannot be ensured simply by making administration accountable to political masters because reaching an agreement with regard to public purposes "can only be partial and incomplete, no matter who is involved"[6]. It means that the administration needs to prepare itself by making use of different techniques to make the assessment of the interests of "vast heterogeneous masses composing the people"[7]. It is difficult, if not impossible, to state with precision what the policy in any given field is at any particular time. Therefore, it follows as a corollary that Public Policy will often be contradictory and conflicting in its effects upon society. Our mythmakers, of course, remain adamant in proclaiming that this should not be so. It is hard to disagree with them, but we still have to face the question of responsibility, seeing that policy is in fact contradictory and conflicting, who is responsible for what, and to whom?[8]

The administrators are to be responsible to the political masters, public service, and the citizens. Though it appears to be somewhat high sounding but it has been dismissed by the scholars as a rationalisation of bureaucratic power inconsistent with democratic politics. It has been emphasised that for imposing clear public purposes on administrators, there is need to champion the political reform for ensuring the institutions to reflect public good. "The improvement of the quality of political parties and elections is to provide a remedy for the ambiguity which gives rise to administrative discretion[9].

It is a fact that administrative responsibility is required to safeguard "Public Interest". Loss of confidence in the ability of the administrators to discern the interest of the public at large would constitute a serious problem in seeking a responsible administration. Over the years, there has developed a feeling that basic civic mindedness has gone away giving way to pursuance of self-interest rather than public interest. Frederickson, commenting upon the commitment to the idea of public service, said, "virtually all our institutions seem to be in trouble. The family is deteriorating, schools seem to be ineffective, there is deep suspicion of most large-scale organisations including industry, business, and government. There is dwindling support for churches. Crime is alarmingly common. We are balkanized into racial, economic, ethnic, demographic and sexual divisions. Privatism, greed, self interest and self-indulgence challenge the notion of community".[10]

Frederickson and Hart have said that there is a threat to

Public Administration due to the rise of values which are more suited to the needs and requirements of business administration and public service is losing its distinctively public character alongwith its historical mission as a means to accomplish community purposes.[11] As per Frederickson, without a strong sense of community, Public Administration will continue to constitute a threat for the citizens and a scapegoat for elected officials.[12] Administrative responsibility just cannot be ensured unless administration not only shows but also means its interest for the public. Commenting upon it Gawthorp said, "In addition to ensuring that the laws are faithfully executed, it must also become the primary responsibility of the permanent career public service, at all levels of government, to ensure the vitality of citizenship in an active citizenry fully engaged in the art of government"[13]

Looking at any facet or theory of administrative responsibility, one point of consensus emerges that the willingness on the part of administration to consider and act on obligations to the citizens is of greatest possible importance and significance. Administrative responsibility is not possible unless each and every functionary in the administration individually: [14]

i) recognises the moral implications of administrative discretion;
ii) understands properly the demands and requirements of his organisation, hierarchical superiors, interest groups, elected representatives, service codes and ethics, and the citizens; and
iii) is in position to take a decision with regard to the significance and relevance of each decision in a specific and particular situation.

Administrative Accountability

In any organisational set-up each and every incumbent has a specified role to perform and render account of it to the superior to whom he is legally accountable in the vertical order of the organisation he is serving in. It is the duty of the superior to allocate the tasks in a manner whereby its accomplishment is ensured through performance by one to whom it has been allocated to and who is accountable for the same to his superior. Every office order or instructions germinating from the top to the bottom and intermediate levels are supposed to inculcate the necessity of accounting for the official or the work assigned to him. The concepts of accountability and responsibility have been treated distinctly by some of the scholars. Mainly the distinction has been focused on the task assigned to a functionary by a superior in terms of control exercised over the junior. Accountability is more of a departmental technique. An administrator could be responsible to the legislature, political parties, electorate, etc., but cannot be accountable to them. He could be accountable to the superior in his organisation. The ultimate superior, of course, is accountable to the political executive and through him to the legislature, electorate, etc.

Administrative responsiveness, as a matter of fact has little difference with administrative responsibility and that is in terms of the vast jurisdiction of administrative responsiveness. Administrative responsiveness implies the adaptability and capitalizing on the changes in the system in terms of social, political and economic factors whereas through administrative responsibility such changes which are institutionalied are taken care of. Likewise, administrative accountability is also one of the techniques to make administration more responsive and responsible.

Administrative Responsiveness: Important Forces

In the early part of this Chapter a question was raised whether the administration could be responsive without the help and cooperation of other related institutions/agencies/forces. It is proper to analyse this issue at length here to see the role of administration, local elected bodies, state political executive, non-governmental organisations/voluntary organisations, pressure groups, and citizens, in making administration responsive. The role of physical environment in making the task of administration in tune with responsiveness would also be analysed. Figure-I shows the interaction between different forces/ factors in making the administration responsive.

Figure-I

Interaction between different forces in making Administration Responsive

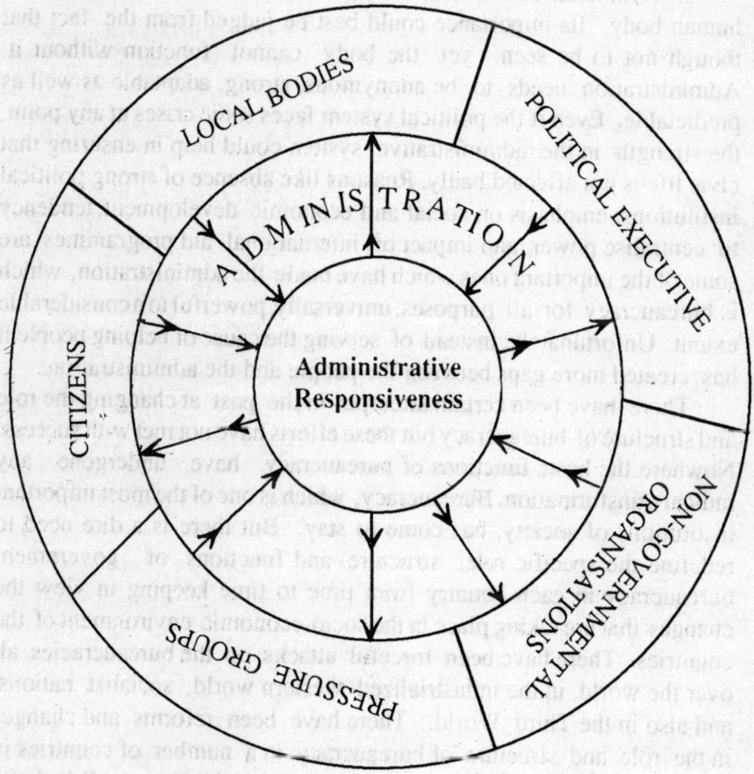

As shown in Figure-I, various forces interact with administrative system and vice-versa and with the help and cooperation of all could make the administration responsive. Moreover through administrative responsiveness even the functioning of various forces could be positively improved in the overall interest of all.

Role of Bureaucracy

Governmental administrative system is like the skeletal system in a human body. Its importance could best be judged from the fact that though not to be seen, yet the body cannot function without it. Administration needs to be anonymous, strong, adaptable as well as predictable. Even if the political system faces some crises at any point, the strength in the administrative system could help in ensuring that civic life is not affected badly. Reasons like absence of strong political institutions, emphasis on social and economic development, tendency to centralise power, and impact of international aid programmes are some of the important ones which have made the administration, which is bureaucracy for all purposes, universally powerful to a considerable extent. Unfortunately, instead of serving the cause of helping people it has created more gaps between the people and the administration.

There have been certain attempts in the past at changing the role and structure of bureaucracy but these efforts have not met with success. Nowhere the basic functions of bureaucracy have undergone any radical transformation. Bureaucracy, which is one of the most important institutions of society, has come to stay. But there is a dire need to redefine the specific role, structure, and functions of government bureaucracy in each country from time to time keeping in view the changes that are taking place in the socio-economic environment of the countries. There have been forceful attacks on the bureaucracies all over the world, in the industrialized western world, socialist nations, and also in the Third World. There have been reforms and changes in the role and structure of bureaucracy in a number of countries in the form of growth of corporatism, rise of adhocracy, political inroads into administrative citadels, community seizure of social services, rise of non-governmental organisations, increasing thrust of privatization and marketization of government functions, etc. But these trends, mainly because of lack of interaction with each other, instead of bringing about reforms in the bureaucracy towards making it more 'client-centred', have rather made it stronger keeping it 'away from people'. It has been felt that bureaucratisation is a functional necessity, as a response to change in the complexity and size of the task rather than an ideological response to problems of society. If there is one character which is very familiar to citizens in all countries, it is a bureaucrat. It won't be wrong to mention that no proper alternative has been found for bureaucracy's basic functions. But it is sad and frustrating to find that the most intelligent lot, which gets inducted into the bureaucratic system, primarily hailing from the same section or sub-sections of the society, is unable or unwilling to work in accordance with the needs and demands of the hour and people. It is unfortunate that things are not happening the way they should ultimately leading to the development of citizens' mistrust and lack of faith in the administration. It is the citizens alone who are the most important resource of any nation and unless they have faith and trust in the administration, their complete and unflinching support, involvement and commitment to the developmental and regulatory activities of the state could not be solicited. Despite the best efforts having been made by the governments at the top echelons of power to make administration at the grassroots more responsive, the net result has not been all that encouraging. It goes without saying that the best technological advancements and well-talked of management techniques and administrative skills could not add qualitatively to the administration's credit to boast about its responsiveness to the citizens who have been rather constrained to develop the feeling that the administration is unfair, unethical, corrupt, and whimsical. It won't be wrong to say that it is a global phenomenon but one could find the laxity and lack of responsiveness on the part of administration more in developing nations. An important reason for this could be lack of positive and meaningful interaction between administration and local institutions and administration and non-governmental organisations. The strength or weakness of these bodies viz., local institutions and non-governmental organisations and their interaction with or lack of the same could help or stand in the way of administration in building responsiveness.

Role of Political Executive

Bureaucracy has a substantive role to play in the administrative scenario. With regard to bureaucracy's role in democracy, it has been argued by Etzioni-Halevey that it is "problematic because this is precisely one of the areas in which the democratic rules of the game are ill-defined, ambiguous, self-contradictory and controversial[15]. It has been made to believe that bureaucracy is supportive as well as antagonistic to democracy. Nevertheless, the importance of bureaucracy cannot be minimised more so in developing societies. The emergence of overpowering bureaucracies in such societies has become a fact of life. With regard to making the bureaucracy or administration responsive to the needs, demands, expectations and aspirations of the system as well as its constituents in the form of citizens, bureaucracy depends to a large extent on the political executive to which it is subordinated because the political executive derives authority from the electorate whereas bureaucracy draws its strength from the administrative positions and the rules, regulations and policies enacted by the political executive from time to time. Though the role performed by bureaucracy in policy formulation cannot be denied, yet the ultimate credit or discredit for the execution of policies goes to the political executive. Not only the enactment of sound policies but also making available the requisite environment for the administration to implement those policies become the duty and utmost obligation of the political executive because it is they in whom the ultimate power resides and who have the mandate of the people to govern. Efforts to pursue the attainment of specified goals and targets, appropriate and positive use of discretion and respect for rules and regulations on the part of the political executive are some of the key areas to be taken care of by the political executive. The political executive, because of its enormous powers, can make as well as stand in the way of making administration responsive. Misutilization of position, unnecessary harassment of administration and inappropriate use of discretion for pursuing self-interest are some of the important factors which de-motivate the bureaucracy and widen the gap between political and permanent executives ultimately affecting the performance of administration affecting the interests of the common man . Political executive, if it portrays itself to be a model of ''best governors'' could make administration accomplish its task for the benefit of all in the best possible manner. Occasionally, the people on jobs in administration consider themselves to be handicapped and tools in the hands of political executives and feel that they are made to dance to the tune of political executives. This is a major aspect which the political masters must take serious note of. The technical expertise and administrative acumen of the bureaucracy, acquired by their long service, could best be made use of by the political executive in case they act in a fair and impartial manner and away from their ''self-interests''.

The political executive can help in making the administration responsive, if apart from the points discussed above, the political executive plays a role in providing a representative, balanced, and participatory bureaucracy, because for all purposes the major onus for bringing an element of responsiveness in the administration lies with bureaucracy. A representative bureaucracy is one which "consists of reasonable cross-section of the body politic in terms of occupations, class, geography and the like, and must be in general tune with the ethos and attitudes of the society of which it is a part[16]. The success of any democratic system depends to some extent on the representative character of the civil service. This enables the bureaucracy to operate in accordance with the established values, attitudes and ethos of the society being an integral part of the system. The political executive could make policies to bring about a representative bureaucratic force. Besides being representative, bureaucracy needs to be in a state of balance in order to be integrated completely into the fabric of a democratic regime. In the words of Nachmias and Rosenbloom, "A bureaucracy is in imbalance when it fails to operate on the basis of democratic consent. Bureaucratic imbalance may be either despotic or subservient. Despotic implies that the bureaucracy is too much the master while subservient implies that it is too much the servant[17]. These scholars have further stated that the balance of this kind of bureaucracy consists of: (a) widespread knowledge about the bureaucracy; (b) a sense of feeling that public interests are being served by the bureaucracy; and (c) bureaucracy has adequate prestige value and provides equal treatment to all.[18] A representative and balanced bureaucracy can make the element of responsiveness of administration reflect positively and become participatory. Participatory bureaucracy is one which has : (a) high degree of social representativeness; (b) organisational democracy; (c) permission to the bureaucrats to freely contribute to the debate in public on issues of public policy; and (d) participation of citizens in bureaucratic decision making.[19] Participatory bureaucracy would make itself more politically responsive and also more efficient in its performance of the targeted tasks. Of course, making bureaucracy representative, balanced and participatory could be possible if the political executive wish to make it so. One thing which clearly emerges out of this is that such action on the part of political executive for re-orienting the basics and structure of bureaucracy would capacitate administration to be more awakened, enlightened, strong, capable, and responsive not only to the citizens but also to the system and the society at large. Besides playing a major role in restructuring bureaucracy, as explained above, the political executive has an important task in helping and smoothening the performance of administration through day-to-day functioning and the modus-operandi of the political executive vis-a-vis bureaucracy, citizens, and the system.

Political masters, as stated earlier, do enjoy the confidence of people. They can play an enormously important part in making the citizens behave in a manner conducive to the appropriate functioning of the administration. This is possible, on their part, by setting ideal precedents, restraining from exercising their authority inappropriately, avoiding uncalled for pressures on administration, cooperating with the bureaucracy; and discarding undemocratic and unethical practices.

Role of Local Institutions

The local institutions are meant to cater to the needs of the inhabitants and particular areas covered by them. In the local institutions, people take upon them the major responsibility of development in their area through the locally elected representatives. It is thus a system wherein institutional arrangements are made to achieve development through the initiative and participation of the local population. The local institutions are also considered nurseries for political democracies providing active support as a watch-dog to the administration at work in the local areas.

The performance of the local institutions whether with regard to providing experienced legislators and parliamentarians, acting as an agent for ushering in social, economic or cultural development, or providing support/checking agency to the work of the administration, is not satisfactory qualitatively.

It has been observed, over the years, that local institutions at the grassroots, for example, Municipal Committees and Municipal Corporations in urban areas in India, and Gram Panchayats, Panchayat Samittis, and Zila Parishads in rural areas are too weak. The will of the people is more manifest in Parliament than it is in the Municipal bodies, Gram Sabhas and Zila Parishads, not because there is any inherent weakness but because, at the grassroots levels, elections have not been regular or consistent, State control is enormous, supersession and dissolutions are frequent, and financial strength and autonomy are negligible. What has been seen is long and frequent spells of non-representative local governments. The requirement is to develop and strenghten these local bodies and to flush out the connections between representative governments and administration so that working with active support of each other the administration could be more responsive. Because of the weak local institutions, the representatives of these bodies have started working rather negatively when viewed in the context of building of administrative responsiveness. They approach the administration for tasks of their favoured ones and it provides a handle to the administration to do whatever it feels like because it is known to the local bureaucracy that the so-called local institutions' leaders cannot raise a finger at its activities. The strengthening of local bodies and performance of a positive role by them could do wonders while working together with the administration. It cannot be denied that the nature of relationship between the political leaders and organisations and administration has a very significant bearing on systematic goal-gratification in any given politico-administrative polity especially at the grassroots (e.g., District and below in India) because these are the basic territorial units of administration as well as political organisations. It is here that the law and order is maintained, facts for policy formulation are collected, and developmental plans are implemented. These organisations and the administration at this level having a finger in the pie could do an excellent job of building administrative responsiveness. May be the administrators find it difficult to carry the commoners among citizens alongwith their functional mechanism and clearly explain administration's constraints and handicaps to them but the representatives of the political organisations being one of the citizens and, to a considerable extent by enjoying the confidence of the people, could mould the citizens in extending a helping hand to the administration amounting to qualitative administrative responsiveness. Moreover, the strongly activated local institutions, depending upon the need of the local areas, could impress upon the administration the need to work effectively and efficiently on the problems and work priorities tabled before the administration by such local institutions.

Role of Non-Governmental Organisations

With passage of time, not only the governmental functions have increased manifold but also the citizens' dependence on administration for all the works has gone up substantially. For every thing, big or small, people have developed a tendency to look towards the administration. It won't be wrong to say that all this has led to an utter confusion in the administration for not being specifically aware of what to do and what to leave. Besides political executive and local institutions, there is enough need to have in operation other supplemental and alternative channels which could be assigned some responsibility presently being undertaken by the administration.

Non-governmental organisations (NGOs) could play an important role in shedding and sharing some of the work being accomplished by or on the task-agenda of the administration. As is clear from the nomenclature, the NGOs are private organisations but are somewhat different than what generally is referred to as private sector. The NGOs are registered as trusts or societies consequent upon which they are, unlike private sector organisations, not to earn profits. These organisations have their focus on developmental programmes, like health, nutrition, family planning, education, water supply, sanitation, urban renewal, slum clearance, etc. Normally, the private sector abstains from undertaking such activities more so when the element of profit making is not the motive at all. Sizeable number of NGOs, more true in case of rural areas, undertake governmental programmes[20] on a contractual basis.

Over the past decade, non-governmental organisations have become prominent actors in the development field, where they are perceived to be able to do something that national or state governments cannot or will not do. Government bureaucracies in most of the Third World countries have failed to provide satisfactory services to the poorest in the society and have not been effective in realizing most of the objectives like poverty eradication, rural development and child health care programmes. Besides helping the bureaucracy in reducing its workload by taking it on to themselves (NGOs) and leaving enough time with the administration to work speedily in the interest of and for the benefit of the people, the NGOs with their effective and positive working could keep a check on the functioning of the administration and could also act as an evaluator of the administration's day-to-day work performance for the purpose of providing well-meant feedback to it for improvement.

Role of Pressure Groups

Pressure groups are organised interest groups in which members share common views and objectives and actively carry on programmes to influence governmental functionaries and the system. These groups are primarily interested in influencing the determination and operation of government policies and programmes, which are carried out by the administration that directly or indirectly affect their members. These groups come into existence in different forms under distinct circumstances.

As stated above, the basic purpose of a pressure group is to attempt to protect the interests of its member/members. What the interest could be? It could be somewhat personal and suitable to the need of a distinct group. What is the overall interest of the society at large vis-a-vis the administration? Obviously, the performance by the administration conducive to the societal norms, values, ethics, and governmental rules, regulations, and policies. In case the pressure groups think positively on the mode of administrative operations, probably the groups could not only help the administration to perform in the best possible manner but could also mobilize public opinion in favour of the administration for making it more responsive to the needs of all concerned. Fighting out with the administration by the pressure groups for seeking their own, not so important, ends when viewed in the total scenario, and contradicting each other would provide ample leverage to the administration to make the best use of these groups and their activities suiting the ends of the administration away from the majority of the inhabitants' interests. Because of their organisational capabilities and strengths, rather the pressure groups could stand shoulder to shoulder with the administration and facilitate the same to perform in a called for manner.

Role of Citizens

Citizen is an individual who is a native or naturalised member of a state, owes allegiance to it, and is entitled to the protection and privileges of its laws. Thus, a citizen is one who has a status in the governmental system. It is the obligation of the administration to provide for his basic necessities. Especially, in a democratic polity, the citizen is to be cared for the most. There are civil, military and para-military forces to not only protect him from all dangers and threats to life but also to make his living comfortable.

What is apparent on the Indian scene at the moment is that the gap between citizens and administration is widening more and more every day. The feeling of being unsafe and insecure in the hands of administration is getting strength and becoming more deep-rooted. The citizens have been convinced that the administration is lethargic, inefficient and corrupt and unless they make use of some unhealthy practice, their work won't be carried out. There is complete mistrust in the administration. They feel that rules and procedures in accordance with which the administration works are quite complicated and lengthy. For getting even the simplest thing done, the issue has to be in the pipeline for quite a substantial amount of period and what the result even then would be is not very clear. If the citizens complain, their complaints/grievances are not sorted out or redressed. The citizens who have the right to elect the political executives whom the administration is subordinated to, in fact, should be given due regard but the picture is quite dark. The administration is at the giving end and the citizens at the receiving end.

The questions arise : What is the way out?; could the administration take care of all the things adequately and to the satisfaction of all concerned without the active support of the citizens? or, how the citizens could help make the administration responsive?

The way out is an active cooperation between citizens and administration. Administration is to serve the public and it could be improved if citizens also cooperate with it and attempt to understand and appreciate its problems and constraints. Indian citizens are too much possessive. There is nothing wrong in it. But one should not try to stick to those guns which are contrary to the rules and regulations of the land. An illustration to this effect could be the encroachment which the people belonging to small business community have made to the roadsides. At the cost of traffic rules, municipal regulations and civic amenities, these people are going ahead with their business and whenever they are asked to move away from those sites, they feel that something due and deserving is being snatched away from them by the administration for the purpose of harassing them. Indian society has a peculiar characteristic of heterogeneity and is composed of people hailing from numerous castes, religions, and of different language groups. Because of the long existing feudal set-up in the country more or less the Indians still continue to be a society somewhat akin to the feudalistic pattern This has resulted in moulding the thinking of the people on those lines. Such a character of Indian society manifests itself in patronage, disregard of rules and procedures, authoritative attitudes whether at work in the organisation or in the community. There are very little democratic traditions in our culture despite the fact that India is a democratic polity. Most of the people are ignorant, unaware and almost illiterate. Ignorance and material prejudices, etc., continue to be widespread and lead to an authoritarian mentality and attitude practically at all levels. Especially with the masses, this takes the shape of fatalism. Such traits are thoroughly contrary to a democratic system.

Besides attempting to establish its credibility in the minds of citizens, the administration is required to act as an educator, reformer and change agent. Any kind of mistrust or feeling of snobbery or favourtism in the minds of citizens and administrators towards each other would always stand as an obstacle in the way of establishing a feeling of mutual cooperation and trust. The citizens can play a very important role in making the administration responsive if they start adhering to some moral values and ethics. Besides understanding the problems of administration, the citizens should attempt to refrain from making unjust claims on the administration. For making it work to the best, the administration could draw its major strength from the citizens.

Role of Physical Environment

The environment at the place of work plays an important role in determining the performance of the functionaries. A neat, clean, well laid out office acts as a source of satisfaction not only for the people at work but also for the outside visitors. As discussed earlier, almost every citizen, in one capacity or the other, for one work or the other, has to approach the government offices. Physical infrastructure is of enormous importance in properly arranging the office. Which things are of significance and also their importance vis-a-vis building of administrative responsiveness are discussed in the following paragraphs.

Seating arrangement in the office has to be made in a manner whereby there is an optimum utilisation of the office space, people at their desks are able to work without having a rush of people around them, there are proper stacks for keeping the office record without making the tables of the functionaries crowded with files, etc... Functionaries need to be made to sit in such a way whereby they do not talk with each other all the time and also by which the controlling officer could keep a watch on the functioning in the office. The office should not give the impression that the records lying everywhere have probably never been looked into and whenever the need arises the relevant papers are difficult to be traced. Lot of attention is required to maintain and preserve the records in such a systematic way that whenever any document is required, it is available without delay.

Window or counter system with provision for giving tokens to the various citizens approaching an office minimises the rush of the people around the functionaries. The person once having received the token could be told to go to a specific counter after a stipulated period of time to know about the decision on his request/claim so far as the routine matters are concerned. In case the work has some major implications then the person could be told to come after a few days. Such an arrangement would give the people a sense of satisfaction with the working of the Office.

Important information regarding programmes being executed, targets attained and to be attained must be displayed at an easily approachable place in the office so that people don't have to unnecessarily keep on enquiring. Proper enquiry system set up at the reception counter could help people know the exact official to approach for their work.

Besides, special attention has to be given to keep the office neat, clean, properly whitewashed or, painted. Often one finds the urinals and toilets in the offices extremely dirty. Not only does it make them non-functional, it also leads to foul smell in the total office environment.

All the abovesaid points seem to be very minor but have a great bearing on the functioning of the office and earn dissatisfaction of clients who would think that the administration is not responsive.

Often the heads of the departments and other senior functionaries in the Secretariat, Directorates, Departments at State, District, Sub-division and Block levels say that they don't have adequate finances to provide an appropriate physical environment. This does not hold good because to make the place of work neat, clean and to make arrangements in the office conducive to the work requirements probably does not need as much of finances or other infrastructure as it needs the will to do the same. Proper environment would facilitate the functioning of the administration thus narrowing the ever-widening gap between the citizens and the administration.

An effort has been made in the preceding part to focus on different and important forces which do have or could have a substantive role to perform in making the administration responsive. Clear identification of goals and its follow-up by each such force could mean a lot for providing such type of administrative system which is up to the expectations of majority of the citizens and could cope with the challenges being faced by the system and the society. In the succeeding paragraphs, some of the major challenges being faced by the administration which stand in the way of it being responsive would be discussed to prepare ground to talk about the techniques for making administration responsive in the next chapter.

Administrative Responsiveness: Major Challenges

Every one has a natural desire and instinct to crave for the best possible under any given situation he finds himself in. Keeping in view the attitude and bent of mind of citizens, in a system like that of India, where the dependence on the administration is so much, the public in India would definitely wish to have a sound and well-meant system of administration for coming up to the satisfaction of the society at large. But there are a number of reasons which could be responsible for the lack of responsiveness on the part of the administration. These are:

India on the whole can boast of well-established moral values, ethics, and ethos. Do we have these things existing as such at the present time? More true as answer to it would be in its negation. But it needs some explanation to understand as to why it has happened. Consequent upon long dependence on various kinds of rulers and kingdoms which had been frequently invading the country and ruling it by exploiting its natural as well as human resources, the total thinking of the human beings in the Indian society has been badly affected. The other side of the picture reveals that the general morality which the majority of the society's constituents used to possess, say around five to six decades back, is now at the negative end. Still one finds that there are some such values and moral principles which, as a result of these having been accepted for a long period of time, are persisting in the society. There are still some such precedents which people would not like to do away with. Likewise, there have been some such decisions taken by the administration in the past which people have taken as accepted norms of administration. What one finds now is that as a result of some ego issues or because of certain other compelling forces, the administration and administrators have started losing touch with past traditions and values. Administration needs to develop a rationale and logic for not only the development as such but also to make it acceptable among the people, if one is to place to a side all that is considered now as having outlived its utility. Administration must cherish and nurture such norms which did have and still have value and are being inherited by the people as well as the system. One of the important reasons for the lack of administrative responsiveness is the fact that the administration has started functioning absolutely afresh by doing away even with the just practices, values, and decisions taken in the past. The system must have contact with the past and base its future on it.

Since independence India has witnessed a good amount of growth in almost all the sectors. The industrial growth, green revolution, white revolution, increase in literacy rate, social welfare functions, health care programmes and a number of other related areas have undergone tremendous change for the better. For making the benefits resulting from various developmental and social welfare aspects available to the vastly increasing population the functions of administration have increased to an almost unlimited extent. Besides taking utmost care of development activities, the administration has to perform routine or regulatory administrative tasks as well in the best possible manner. Terrorist and secessionist activities, lawlessness among the society, student unrest, trade union activities, pressures from across the borders, all have made the task zones of administration more complicated. Moreover, the administration's tendency in this country to keep everything under its own shadow is also responsible for it developing almost cold feet in sizeable number of areas. Less number of non-governmental organisations and voluntary associations coupled with Government's lukewarm attitude to the functioning of those in existence is also one of the reasons for the administrative structure and the evolved mechanism being unable to cope with the huge quantum of tasks. The administration is unable to decide as to which areas need priority attention and which do not and what should be the proportion of the same. Such a state of affairs is responsible for the administration not being able to be as responsive as required.

India is completely different from what it used to be in the late 1940s. "Yet a parallel transformation has not taken place in the mental attitudes in our country, in the outlook, in the minds of our people. This perhaps is one of the bigger challenges that we have to face today. There is no excuse to absolve us of the responsibility of giving things a fresh look. We have to assess and review what has happened and, in that light, to bring to bear our experience to the new challenges that lie ahead. We have to apply fresh thinking[21].

As mentioned earlier, the Indians over the centuries had developed, by looking at the governmental systems in operation from time to time, a feeling that administration and governmental functionaries and systems are meant to oppress and suppress the masses. Even after independence this attitude has not undergone much change. People still feel that it is the administration that has the power and authority to do all the things. Furthermore, the way the administrative system has been functioning in India since independence reveals that all the tasks are being performed by the administration. All this has resulted in too much of dependence of the public on the administration alongwith a feeling of awe, and suspicion in their minds towards administration. This mental attitude of the people again poses a great challenge to the administration for being responsive.

There is no denying the fact that civil service or bureaucracy has a key role in getting the benefits to citizens, who are its clients for that matter. Majority of them come in contact with the administration at the cutting edges. After not getting anything positive done there, very few of them take up the courage to approach the top administration or politicians for the purpose of straightening the things. In the existing administrative system where a large number of decisions regarding day to day aspects are to be taken, the powers and authority with such cutting edges of administration are thoroughly limited. Small decision which could be made at that level are being referred to the District/Directorate/ Secretariat levels. Besides, there is overpowering control of top administration over the lower echelons of administration. As a result of this enormous control, check, and lack of authority, power and clarifications of the rules and regulations, the administrative channels at lower levels are unable to keep pace with the time and needs/ demands of the people.

It is with the rules and procedures that the administration performs its various functions. These provide guidelines to the functionaries for sorting out and deciding the cases at their level. Rules, regulations and procedures are meant to deliver the goods effectively and speedily without putting the beneficiaries to loss. Somehow or the other, the rules, regulations and procedures which are made at the controlling levels are becoming more and more complicated and cumbersome for all in the administration and for general public's understanding the same for their proper compliance. The public need to understand the rules and procedures because it would make them appreciate the same and reduce their unnecessary demands which are not in accordance with the rules and regulations. At times there is only one functionary or two in the District and even in the Directorate who know clearly about all the rules and regulations regarding a particular issue. When that official is unable to attend to his duty the whole work stands still. Sets of rules framed at the top are sent to the lower levels. Because of increase in number of functions and number of people directly or indirectly affected by them, no attempt has been made by the administrative functionaries to have a clear and comprehensive understanding of all these rules, some of which even get contradicted by the fresh ones without new rules coming to the notice of the functionaries. Thus decisions made as per old rules would be wrong in nature and spirit. Besides the rules, the administrative procedure is also quite complicated and lengthy. This also stands in the way of quick disposal of cases or demands of the people.

There is no denying the fact that the bureaucracy or the administration enjoy all power and is a potent force. It becomes more powerful when there are technological, specialised, and internationally-aided programmes to be taken care of and especially when the political executive is not that clear, conscientious or strong. In a democratic system, the ultimate power and authority rest with the political executives. When the political masters interfere in the day to day functioning of administration and misutilise their position for getting wrongs done by the administration, the administrative system is crippled. Any one who talks to the politicians will get a response that the administration is not doing its work adequately. Well, the same stands true when an administrator is talked to. All the functions are to be executed by the administration and when the administrative organisations are pressurised by the politicians for favouring any particular person or group of persons in disregard to any rules, regulations, etc., it makes people feel that the administration is unfair and cares only for those who could afford to get political pressure exercised on it. Lack of positive support or cooperation from the political masters stand considerably in the way of responsive orientation of the administration.

Policy making is considered to be more a task of political executive. Of course, it has lately been established that a clear line of demarcation between politics and the administration's role in formulation of policies cannot be drawn, yet the major responsibility of making the policies is that of the political executive with the suggestive, informative and analytical role of and assistance by the permanent executives. In order to justify and to bring to fore the much called for developmental and regulatory activities, large number of policies are being framed. Without sorting out the relevant details, rules, regulations, procedures, infrastructure, and channels for the execution of such formulated policies, the political masters in order to gain popularity propagate the same among the public through all possible sources. As a result of such announcements, people individually and in groups start approaching the administration for getting the needful done in accordance with the policies propagated. The administration feels handicapped on such occasions as it has no details to deal with such demands. People on the other hand develop a feeling that the administration is not helping them out even when such a policy has already been formulated. This creates strains in the relationship between the citizens and administration probably without any fault of either side.

The policy documents issued to the appropriate executing agencies are at times not clearly worded leaving enough scope to speculate about the interpretation of the legal terminology used in the same. Besides, at times the policies framed have some clauses which contradict few others in the same policy or in earlier formulated policies. In such circumstances where the policy document is not clear and needs explanation on some aspects from the top it leads to delay in the implementation of the scheme or policy. This kind of delay is not properly appreciated by the citizens. It gives them an impression that the administration is not interested in safeguarding the citizens' interests.

For execution of any programme or scheme having been formulated by the Government, the administration requires financial resources. Often, it is found that the administrative agencies are already over-worked with the implementation of different programmes and there is hardly any scope left with them to take up the momentous tasks of implementing other policies especially where there is a resource crunch. Administration at lower levels strongly feels that this stands in the way of its implementing activities. On the other hand, the governmental machinery at the top does not attach due importance to this significant aspect and as a result the administrative tasks are jeopardised. Citizens, on the other hand, who are to get the benefits only after the implementation of the policy, feel thoroughly aggrieved and agitated with the administration when they don't find the execution of the programme/scheme with full zeal, enthusiasm and efficiency by the administration. Financial bankruptcy of the administrative agencies poses a challenge to the responsiveness of the administration.

Local institutions can play an active role in making the administration responsive and work in accordance with the needs and interests of the majority of the section of the people whom they represent. Unfortunately, local bodies in India are thoroughly weak and under enormous control of the state governments. Often one finds these local institutions as having either been superseded or dissolved without any definite date for the next elections to be held. There is no denying the fact that Indian institutions of democracy are stronger at higher levels but what also needs to be done is to take care of these democratic institutions at the important place of administration, i.e., the local areas. In the words of Rajiv Gandhi, "the will of the people is more manifest in Parliament than it is in the Gram Sabhas and Zila Parishads, not because there is any inherent weakness but because at the grassroot level, elections have not been regular or consistent. We have acquiesced in long and frequent spells of non-representative local government".[22] Given the situation, local institutions which could perform a fairly important role in strengthening the administration by making people who have confidence in their elected representatives, understand, appreciate and cooperate with the administration, are unable to do because of their low status and position. In one sense, it becomes the duty of the administration also to attempt to strengthen the local bodies in turn to get support from these institutions to make the administration perform smoothly. After all, the administration which is, composed of people hailing from the same society has the responsibility to take up such tasks whereby it could serve the public in the best possible manner. More than it, the local institutions could understand and appreciate the problems and priority areas of work in their respective jurisdictions better than the State or national level institutions. A strong local body could not only keep a check on the functioning of the administration but could also play an important role in making the administration follow up the work in accordance with the needs of the local areas enlisted in a priority order by the local institutions.

There is a very intimate and close relationship between citizens and administration. Citizens are to get every thing pertaining to their life from the administration and the administration is supposed to provide the same to them. The administrators prefer to be called bureaucrats than public servants. This in itself brings to light the attitude of the administrator. At times, one just wonders how the mental make up of an individual changes so fast once he gets inducted into the bureaucracy. It is a common feeling among the citizens that the administrators do not consider themselves as citizens but something much more. On the other hand, the administrators do feel that they are not super human beings and are like any other person in the society. Without the active support of the citizens, political masters and administrative system, the administrators cannot function properly to satisfy the needs, demands and aspirations of all concerned. A word with the administrator in this regard would get the response that the citizen in India has become much more demanding without caring for the problems and constraints faced by the administration. The citizen has the feeling that since he has the right to elect the political masters, he needs to get all the benefits from the administration irrespective of the stipulated rules, regulations and procedures. He wants that his work should be taken up at the top-most priority and done to the best of his interests. No system can work well where the two important constituents of the system, that is, the citizens primarily for whom the system exists, and the administrators who are to work for the system and citizens, have such kind of uncooperative attitude towards each other. Lack of active cooperation and support from the citizenry stand in the way of proper functioning of administration.

Before independence, the people in India had fear and suspicion with regard to the functioning and functional mechanism of the administration. Immediately after the independence, it dawned on them that it is now their own government and thus they can get each and every thing from the government within the minimum possible time. It is normally felt that no individual is ready to seriously take note of his duties and obligations but in turn, is more and more right-conscious. The Indian nationals do have a peculiar characteristic of being individualistic without having any commitment or sense of belonging to the Nation or system as such. A small illustration to this effect could be that we don't mind throwing out the garbage after cleaning our houses on the roadside but certainly would feel thoroughly offended and would curse the system if on the second day the drains are not cleaned. Well, it is difficult to imagine any system functioning where the citizens on the one hand have more and more expectations of the administration, and the administration on the other does have a feeling that it is facing all sorts of problems and constraints to cope with the responsibilities assigned to it. It holds true that in a democratic polity, the citizens' lawfully granted rights have to be protected and through developmental schemes, their socio-economic upliftment has to be pursued but along with it is a rider on the citizens also to first deserve and then aspire for a particular thing. Such attitude of the citizens does not serve any other purpose but to make the administration incapable and incapacitated to come up to the expectations and aspirations of the people ultimately making them develop a feeling that the administration is not responsive.

To usher in development in various areas is the responsibility of the government. In the absence of development, modernisation in life and upliftment of the standard of living cannot come about. The administration has a major role to perform to bring these developmental activities to light. It virtually becomes very difficult for the administration when it comes across distinct vested interests leading to the jeopardising of such developmental activities. The pressure and interest groups who want to attain their vested interests by applying such kinds of tactics are posing a challenge to the administration to seriously take up developmental endeavours.

Where there is will, there is a way. It is an old but proven saying and does mean that when an individual takes it upon himself to do any task he certainly endeavours to make a headway. At times, one does not attain success but it does not imply that all the attempts put forth go in vain. Human being has been gifted with intelligence and thinking capabilities to find out solutions to the problems coming his way. Moreover, when the intelligence level of the administrators is taken into consideration, one finds that they are intelligent and because of that only could enter the civil service through competitive exams. It is hard to believe that the deterioration which is evident in the present day's system is all because of the political influence, lack of active cooperation of the citizens or inappropriate and complicated procedures. To a considerable extent it could be ascribed to the administrators' lack of willingness and inclination, to take up the issues seriously, which hampers the strength of administrative responsiveness. Most of the people in the administration wonder why should they take any initiative. May be it is so because they are afraid of facing direct consequences in case some thing wrong happens and also feel contented by looking at each other meaning thereby that if 'A' and 'B' are not taking any special measures why 'C' should take it up. Due to such uncalled for and unhealthy attitude of the incumbents in administration the deteriorating standards are becoming more and more apparent in the system as well as in the society. As mentioned earlier the citizens are more right conscious, probably the same holds true in case of administrators also. They also want to play safe and to have under their control and accessibility all that is possible for themselves. In such a scenario, the citizens could be excused but certainly not the administrators who relatively have much more responsibility towards the system and society when compared with an ordinary citizen. Basically, to make administration responsible and responsive is the major task of the functionaries in the administration and the others, viz. political executive, citizens, local bodies, etc., are just supplemental organs. In view of this, it becomes more a sacred duty and obligation of the administrators to possess a strong will and desire to do something in a manner wherein the system of administration could claim to have come up to the satisfactory performance level.

Somehow or the other the Indian system got developed with the feeling of fear and suspicion of one element towards the others. The administration feels that the political masters and citizens are not cooperating with it, the politicians have a feeling that administrators do not perform the tasks judiciously and efficiently and the citizens are always at the demanding end. The citizens at the other end are thoroughly dissatisfied with the administration and politicians. It is quite an unhealthy trend and has wider implications for the system and society which is still developing and has yet a long distance to cover. Consequent upon such thinking and feeling towards each other, firstly, none is doing his tasks seriously, secondly, no one takes any special initiative, and thirdly, there is lack of willingness and strong desire to accomplish the targets in a way which shows the responsiveness towards the system. When one talks of responsiveness of the administration, the major focus of attention is on the administrative institutions. The question arises: does the administration, especially at the grassroots or cutting edges, have enough powers and authority to improve upon itself in the direction of making it responsive? An illustration, though of minor importance, could be that a District Magistrate and a Superintendent of Police who are heading the civil and police administration in a district, cannot transfer a 'Patwari' and a 'Constable' respectively in their jurisdiction and when it is done there is political pressure to undo the same. Likewise, there are so many examples which reveal lack of enough powers and authority with the lower rungs of administration. Problems and constraints at one end and lack of willingness to improve or contribute to the improvement of the system at the other stand in the way of each other. Besides these problems, there is substantial resistance from a number of channels to any change sought to be brought in the system. Again even if willing, the administrators are unable to bring in innovations in the system to make it responsible and responsive mainly because of lack of enough powers and authority.

The Indian system of administration has tall organisations instead of flat organisations. There are long hierarchies in the system at every level, Secretariat, Directorate, Division, District, Sub-Division, and

Block. Any paper has to go to almost five to eight levels for a decision and it returns to the functionaries who had moved it in the same order. Such a system results in delay in the work. Any one not available for a day or two would mean detaining the paper at that level. If one takes up sample cases of similar nature from any office, one would find the case having been dealt with by five to seven persons and invariably in all it is the lowest functionary in the hierarchy who moves the case who has written something without anything important, significant, informative, suggestive, and analytical contributed to the same by the channels in between the initiator and the final deciding authority. Such type of long hierarchies stand in the way of efficient and prompt disposal of cases.

Any person joining an organisation has some strong drives, motives and strengths alongwith some urges. Every organisation is basically an association of individuals, who are, by birth, very complex in nature and rarely agree with each other. Every one has a logic to profess his point of view. The difference of opinion among them not only pertains to their ability to perform a given task but is also reflected in their will and desire to accomplish it. In simple words, it depends on how much they are motivated and what efforts have been made in the organisations, they are serving, in boosting their morale. How adequately the individuals can be motivated depends upon their motives, strengths, and system's attitude and response to the same. Motivation and attitudes are closely tied with the concepts of morale and job satisfaction. Motivation and morale are processes of inducing persons to feel the need for certain desired behaviour for attaining efficiency of the organisation. One finds the forces in operation in the administrative system at very low ebb so far as motivating the persons at job in this system is concerned. Incumbents not feeling motivated and with low morale can never be considered as essential ingredients for ushering in the required performance in effective and efficient way. Lack of motivation, low morale, least job satisfaction, improper goal fixation, etc., are some of the factors which stand in the way of seeking an individual's commitment to the system and its various facets to the maximum extent. Unless and until the administrative functionaries are thoroughly committed to the administrative system and the system also realizes and appreciates their contribution and importance, the called for sense of belonging and commitment to the system can never be ensured. No one in the administration feels it to be his duty or task to accomplish a given job in a stipulated time. Incumbents often take things very lightly without the least seriousness on their part. Lack of interest in the working of the system clearly reveals lack of commitment of the functionaries to the system. This poses a great challenge to the system and unless it is improved upon the administrative responsiveness can never be witnessed.

The concept of responsibility has been explained in the earlier section. It is essential for healthy functioning of every organisation that responsibility is fixed on different functionaries. It could be divided into two facets. Firstly, the responsibility which is assigned to the functionary and as such becomes a part and parcel of his duties to undertake the same. Secondly, it is the assumed responsibility which is not assigned by the superiors but is taken up by the incumbent on his own. One rarely comes across persons with the will and desire to assume responsibility in the administrative system. In fact, even the assigned responsibility is also not taken care of seriously. Lack of commitment, low motivation, overall societal and systemic make up, etc., coupled with lack of will and strong desire on the part of incumbents are some of the important reasons for administrators not becoming responsible. It is not wrong to say that there is no clear point where the responsibility lies and every channel wants to push it downside or upside. It leads to almost total confusion in the day-to-day administrative functioning.

It has been mentioned above that there is no proper fixation of responsibility and mostly incumbents wish to shirk the same. Other than the reasons explained above is the important point that the goals and targets are not fixed realistically. Either too much quantitative goals are fixed and that again without taking into consideration the capacity and mental level of the functionary/functionaries to perform the same or required infrastructural support is not provided to him/them for taking care of the same. It keeps the administrative officials in a state of confusion as to what is to be done, what is not to be done, how it is to be done, where it is to be done, and with the help of whom it is to be done.

Another important factor is the lack of respect for a human being and/or his dignity in the minds of the officials. An individual is being treated as a 'file' or a 'case' which is a lifeless thing but is concerning an individual who is a living entity, has some identity and has some sentiments, emotions, needs, desires, compulsions and ego. A person weilding heavy pressure, of the politicians, top administrators or because of his influence is treated with respect and dignity but another common citizen without having any one of the abovesaid 'influencing forces' with him is not recognised at all. It is quite important an aspect and could be put into force by the administrators without facing any financial or infrastructural constraints as the lack of it only widens the gap between the common citizen and administration.

Summing up : In this section an attempt has been made to understand the meaning, need and significance of the term 'administrative responsiveness'. Factors responsible for building responsiveness of administration and those making it non responsive have also been discussed. Further, some of the important challenges to administrative responsiveness have been examined. This total framework would enable us to understand and appreciate some of the techniques to be made use of mainly by the administration in the subsequent Chapter.

References

1. Gandhi, Rajiv, "Responsive Administration" Speeches made by Rajiv Gandhi in Workshops of District Magistrates and Collectors, New Delhi, Government of India Press, New Delhi, p. 1.
2. Gandhi, Rajiv, ibid., pp. 11-123.
3. Frederickson, George H., *New Public Administration*, Alabama, University of Alabama Press, 1986, p. 55.
4. Friedrich, C.J., "Public Policy and the Nature of Administrative Responsibility", in C.J. Friedrich and E.S. Masons (eds.), *Public Policy*, Cambridge, Harvard University Press, 1940, pp. 3-4.
5. Tiwari, S.R., "Values in Administration", in Ramesh K. Arora and C.V. Raghavulu (eds.), *Values in Administration*, New Delhi, Associated Publishing House, 1989.
6. Friedrich, C.J., op. cit., p.3.
7. Friedrich, C.J., op. cit., p.24.
8. Friedrich, C.J., op. cit., p.5.
9. Finer, H., "Administrative Responsibility in Democratic Government", *Public Administration Review*, 1940, pp. 335-350.
10. Frederickson, H.G., "The Recovery of Civism in Public Administration", *Public Administration Review*, 1982, pp. 501-508.
11. Frederickson, H.G. and D.K. Hart, "The Public Service and the Patriotism of Benevolence", *Public Administration Review*, 1985, pp. 547-553.
12. Frederickson, H.G., op. cit., 1982, p. 505.
13. Gawthrop, L.C., "Civis, Civitas, and Civilitas: A new focus for the year 2000", *Public Administration Review*, 1984, pp. 101-107.
14. Jos, Philips., "Administrative Responsibility Revisited", *Administration*

and Society, 1990, p. 239.
15. Etizioni - Havley, *Bureaucracy and Democracy*, London, Routledge and Kegan Paul, 1940, p.13.
16. Van Riper, Paul P., quoted in Dwivedi, O.P., and R.B. Jain, *India's Administrative State*, Gitanjli Publishing House, New Delhi, 1985, p. 38.
17. Nachmias, David and David H. Rosen Bloom, *Bureaucratic Culture : Citizens and Administration in Israel*, London, Croom Helm, 1978, pp. 39-40.
18. Ibid., p. 171.
19. Ibid., pp. 183-96.
20. Duggal, Ravi, "NGOs, Government and Private Sector in Health", *Economic and Political Weekly*, March 26, 1988.
21. Gandhi, Rajiv, op. cit., p.1.
22. Gandhi, Rajiv, op. cit., p.11.

2

Some Techniques

A comparison of the present time with the long history of India going back to approximately five thousand years reveals an important point that Indians are free citizens now. It is a unique privilege being enjoyed by the inhabitants of India in the contemporary period. Indians were never free citizens earlier and were only 'Praja' meaning subjects or children being looked after authoritatively and whimsically by the kings, rulers, and governors. In an independent country, the individual having been guaranteed constitutional status of a citizen would not like to be treated by the government officials and administration as a "useless object".

He deems it to be his right to be heard properly and his claims being effectively dealt with by the administration. The sea-change in the 'demanding attitude' appeared on the scene immediately after the independence of the country in 1947. Besides the rise in citizens' expectations, the pressure on the administration also became heavy on account of development activities to be taken care of. Earlier it was performing the routine administration or regulatory administration; now it has in its fold new unpredictable tasks or problems resulting in rapid change in the environment. It was difficult to respond to the demands of the society and the system in the 1950s because the administration did not have enough resource infrastructure appropriate techniques, and skills at that time. Yet the administration's attitude towards the common citizens still remains almost as it was in the1950s whereas the number of administrative functionaries, their development to cope with the tasks, and its resources have increased manifold since then. One does not find the required change in the attitude of the administration as far as its dealing with the human beings is concerned. In the succeeding text some of the techniques which the administration should make use of for making it responsive have been analysed.

Planning

A good number of tasks undertaken by the administration fail to achieve adequate success mainly because there is lack of planning. In its broadest sense, planning means systematic preparation for action. It means some conscious or unconscious preparation that is required to cope with any work or programme which has not emerged on the scene suddenly. Planning in administration means taking stock of the work to be accomplished in a given time frame and restructuring the organisation and its various resources in accordance with the task in such a manner that optimum results could be attained within a stipulated period. The planning of the tasks is very important because it would not only get the tasks accomplished in time but would also amount to reduction in wastage, and avoid crises and a breakdown of the total operation. Not only internal preparation is required, a proper understanding of the task, the area, the target group for which it is to be undertaken has also to be made by all involved in that process. An overall plan document for all the work at hand has to be prepared and the Master Plan must be supplemented by sub-plan documents with regard to each and every work. Likewise, the long-range and short-range planning has to be chalked out properly without giving scope to any individual taking up the liberty to mould the things according to his whims and fancies. In a wider sense, all the different elements of POSDCORB are to be taken serious note of while planning on the part of administrative agencies. It becomes more complicated when it is to be taken care of by the lower levels of the administration which are the ones where the majority of the people come in contact with the administration and where the actual functioning of the administration gets reflected thus leaving its positive or negative imprints on the minds of the people.

The major task of the administration, especially at cutting edges, is to execute the policies of the government from time to time. An illustration of the possible use of planning for any such case could have seven distinct phases, viz: preparation, organisation, scheduling, execution, monitoring, evaluation, and improvements.

Preparation

Whenever any policy is formulated it is passed on to the executing agencies in the form of a policy statement. Often there are a number of points that need to be clarified on the part of the administrative agencies before putting the policy to actual implementation. The doubts should be clarified and legal terminologies used in the policy statement must be thoroughly understood by the concerned agency before the policy is put for implementation. Besides seeking comprehensiveness on the policy statement, the planner at the executing level must get himself thoroughly acquainted with the target area and the target group falling under his functional jurisdiction. It would enable him to foresee the problems and difficulties and possible help he could get from the relevant quarters thus facilitating smooth execution of the policy.

Organisation

Once there is clarity about the policy statement, target area and group, the executor would be competent to lay his hands on the kind and quantity of resources required for executing the policy. The quantum of work to be accomplished in a given period of time would enable him to enlist the manpower, financial and infrastructural requirements. Administration of any programme cannot be efficient without the cooperation of the number of functionaries to be involved in it. Thus an organised body or sub-system would be required to accomplish the task. The designing and building of the administrative structure, which is planning the scheme of the structure and fixing appropriate functionaries to take care of the work, would be done up by jotting down a sub-organisation within the existing organisation of the concerned administration agency. This sub-organisation would be connecting the various parts with every other part having functions, act, office or relation to the whole. The tasks would be divided to eliminate any confusion among the functionaries. A clear chart of resources required would also bring to notice the shortage of resources at hand so that the requisition for the same could be made to the higher levels for speedy work.

Scheduling

Declaration of a policy and it being passed on to the administration for execution make the beneficiaries restless for seeking the benefits through it at the earliest. In planning the execution of a policy, the third important step has to be with regard to the time frame in which the majority of the beneficiaries could secure their claims.

The scheduling needs to be made keeping in view the number of functionaries available, finances, infrastructure, and the size and kind of clientele to be served. While scheduling, feasible target fixation which possibly could be achieved in the light of available resources should always be kept in mind.

Execution

A proper scheme of executing the policy, keeping in view all the pros and cons, should first be made and then the work allotted to various functionaries. The officials involved must be made to understand the policy statement, target area, target groups, targets to be achieved and the time allotted for achieving the targets. This could best be taken care of by the head of the administrative agency as he already has knowledge of all these facets. The officials engaged in the implementation must be made responsible for the work allocated to them with clear instructions to achieve results in the given time.

Monitoring

While planning for the execution programme, the administrative agency having the responsibility must identify the effective way to monitor the total progress so that wherever required it could check the loopholes in the given situation.

Evaluation

There should be scope for a proper evaluation of the execution work so that the erring functionaries could be checked upon in time and extra resources wherever required could be made available.

Improvements

Right in the very beginning when the plan paper is being prepared, the planner must leave enough scope for ushering in improvements in the planned work once it is in the offing. Once all the various stages are well thought over then only the work of implementing the given policy should be taken up. It would leave the things to chance to a very little extent and would rather help the functionaries and the administrative agency to plug the deficiencies not only in time but even before time. Unless and until the work to be undertaken is adequately planned, the chances of the same getting delayed and number of un-anticipated obstructions standing in its way will always be there. Such an effort on the part of administration would enable it to perform the task not only efficiently but effectively as well.

These days one rarely finds an administrative organisation, especially at the grassroots making detailed planning for achieving the targets with regard to any policy passed on to it for implementation. Lack of proper vision, understanding, and planning stand in the way of administration's performing routine and other related tasks as well. From the administration's point of view it could be said that frequent transfers, lack of resources, political interference, lack of citizens' co-operation, etc., are the major factors which stand in their way of planning the work. This certainly has some weight and importance but is not of such great significance that it could prevent the administrators from planning their work well in advance and moving in accordance with the same.

Leadership

In making the administration responsive to the needs, expectations, and aspirations of the citizens, society and the system, much depends on the administrative leadership. The bent of mind, the attitude, the inclination, and the will of the leader will make him and through him his team or subordinates to pursue things accordingly. It is an image of action coupled with power and authority. Leadership is said to be the contribution of personal attributes respected by others, that enables an administrator to share the behaviour of the group being led by him in such a direction which gets determined by the values possessed by the leader.

Commitment, understanding and determination with regard to the tasks to be accomplished make an administrator a responsible leader. These elements play a role in blending together the selfhood of the administrator and the identity of the governmental organisation. A responsible leader in a governmental system must transcend his specialisation. The major traits of a responsible leader in administration could be summarized under two categories: opportunism avoidance and utopian avoidance. Opportunism is the pursuit of immediate, short-run advantages in a way inadequately controlled by considerations of principle and ultimate consequence. To take advantages of opportunities is to show that one is alive, but administrative organisations no less than persons must look to the long-run effects of the present advantage. Opportunism also displays itself in a narrow self-centredness, in an effort to exploit other groups for immediate short-run advantages. A responsible administrative leader recognises the need for stable relations with the community of which his organisation is a part, although he must test the environment to see how real is this requirement. If opportunism goes too far in accepting the dictates of a reality principle, utopianism aims at avoiding hard choices by a flight to abstractions. This too would result in irresponsibility and an escape from the true functions of administrative leadership. A responsible leader will steer the course between opportunism and utopianism. His responsibility will consist of accepting the obligation of providing direction instead of merely ministering to organisational equilibrium; in adopting aspiration to the character of the organisation, bearing in mind that what the organisation has been will affect what it can be and do; and in transcending bare organisational survival by seeing that specialised decisions do not weaken or confuse the distinctive identity of the organisation.[1]

Like any other organisation, a dynamic and effective leadership is required in administration for the overall success of its organs. It is the activity of influencing people to strive willingly for the overall objectives.[2] Leadership is an interpersonal influence exercised in a situation and directed through the communication process toward the attainment of a specialised goal or goals.[3] It has been pointed out that leadership is influencing people to follow in line with the achievement of a common goal.[4] An extensive survey of a large number of studies on leadership was conducted on the basis of which a classification of personal factors associated with leadership was made. It includes: Capacity (intelligence, alertness, verbal ability, originality, judgement); Achievement (scholarship, knowledge, accomplishments); Responsibility (activity, sociability, co-operation, adaptability, humour); Status (socio-economic position, popularity); and Situation (mental level, status, skills, needs, and interests of followers objectives to be achieved, etc.).[5]

The personal factors, as stated above, required in a leader could go a long way in improving the administrative functioning and achieving the goal targets not only in time but also to the satisfaction of the majority of clients. The capacity factor in an administrator would enable him to perceive things in right earnest. Intelligence and verbal ability are two important ingredients of this factor. It goes without saying that most of the administrative organisations are controlled either by incumbents having cleared IAS or State Civil Services examinations through open and tough competitions. On the basis of their intelligence and logical capacity these people could clear the tests and satisfy the members of the selection committees for their induction in the services. Thus their intelligence and verbal ability or expression has to be up to the required mark. These qualities, if coupled with alertness to the tasks, situation, and overall system would make the leader in an administrative agency the originator of new ideas with clear vision about the events to take place in accordance with such original or innovative ideas. The administrators, if having traits, viz: sociability, co-operation, and adaptability, would make them not only responsible in their actions but also responsive in their deeds. The status enjoyed coupled with the advantageous situations (the administrators are mostly in the government service) by the administrative leaders can do wonders in improving the situation by virtue of their intelligence, responsibility, and willingness to work for the pursuance of the best possible.

It is essential for the administrative leaders to possess adequate ability to supervise the work and the work force under their control. The ability to supervise is the most important characteristic for administrative success. By it is meant effective supervision and not quite close, minute and disciplined supervision at all times. Such a trait in an administrator would not only make his organisation keep pace with the quantum of work but also ensure quality output.[6]

The leader holds the prime place in his organisation whether public or private. Majority of the functionaries in organisations have the tendency to work as the leader works. He is a goal-setter and an ideal for the majority of the work force. An administrative leader must reveal his capacity to initiate and innovate things. The trait of initiative has two aspects, motivational and cognitive. The motivational aspect revolves around taking action without any stimulation whereas the cognitive aspect is concerned with problem-finding and opportunity-finding. The administrators initiating things must prepare themselves in advance for the outcomes of their plans and must be capable of visualising better lines of action and execution as per the approved plan.

There is no denying the fact that successful leaders are those who have some personal traits of high quality and merit. But leadership is not a static but a dynamic process implying situations varying in complexities to be dealt with by the leaders. The situational approach to leadership contends that the administrative leaders may not be possessing all the traits to deal with different situations, different followers, and different set of people coming in contact with the administration. So, depending upon the situation the leader should determine his style. Again it brings one to an important question: is it possible to think about a style of leadership to be adopted without having basic intelligence and comprehension? Probably, a mix of the traits and demands of the situation when viewed together would equip an administrator with the capacity to adhere to a suitable functional style.

A number and a variety of roles are to be performed by the leaders of administrative organisations. Besides being an executive, planner, policy maker, group representative, arbitrator and mediator, which are his primary roles,[7] a leader in administration has to be exemplary, a symbol of the team or group, a father figure and a scapegoat as part of accessory roles.[8] More than that, the leader in an administrative system ought to be one who has a clear knowledge about his group, his clients, his jurisdictional area and the type of the particular political environment.

Impoverished, Country Club, Task, Middle of the Roader, and Team have been described as five styles of leadership by Blake and Mouton. In the style 'Team' there is the leader's high concern for people and there is interdependence through a 'common stake' in organisation which amounts to a relationship of trust and respect.[9] Simply having great concern for work or for relations distinctly would probably not serve the purpose of an administrator. He should not only, through his actions, make a friendly atmosphere of belonging, oneness, trust, and respect in the organisation but should also have in mind utmost concern for the work, the targets, and the effective mechanism for the attainment of the same.

Depending upon the situation, the administrator should adhere to the administrative style. Under situations where people in the organisation are to be developed for the accomplishment of the targets, the style should be oriented more towards relationship and less towards work. Contrary to it, when the administrator as a leader is clear what needs to be done with regard to a given aspect and how it should be done without leaving any scope for resentment, the administrator may act as a benevolent autocrat because it would curtail the delay in achieving the goal.[10] One can never minimise the importance of human concern for the administrator but it should be put to use where it is required and certainly not at the cost of the work. All the time an administrator acting as a missionary and having high relationship and low task orientation, especially in situations where subordinates are already developed and work is required to be performed effectively, is not welcomed. Moreover the administrator should never give the impression that he is a 'deserter' having low concern both for relations and work.[11] He should never appear to be passive and uninvolved. Using authority and autocracy also, especially when it is not called for, makes an administrator ineffective. He should attempt not to reveal that he has no confidence in others and is interested only in the work and the same to be carried out as he wishes.[12]

In the preceding text an attempt has been made to explain what the leader should do in administration for the effective functioning of his organisation. Mentioned below are some of the points which could assist the administrators in given situations.

In this situation, the incumbent heading an organisation or agency of government administration has been recently posted on this position. He should keep a low profile in the beginning and attempt to fully understand the various aspects of the organisation -- the human element, the targets, and the resources--before making up his mind to select the line of action to be made use of. He should not take decisions in haste which prove to be wrong and he, later on, has to either withdraw them or get alongwith them to satisfy his ego. It would result into utter failure of the organisation. By virtue of his intelligence and past service experience, the administrator must try to analyse the given situation in the organisation and what needs to be done has to be evolved in a phased manner.

Mention has been made of the 'Developer' style of the leader. Under situations when an altogether new policy or programme has been passed on to the administrative agency for execution, or the situation where the functionaries involved in the office work are highly oriented to rules and procedures and would not budge an inch here or there, or the situations where the citizens, in the shape of the client group, do not want to understand and appreciate the problems of the administration, it becomes the duty of the leader in the set-up to act as a 'Developer'. He must adhere to high relationship--and low task-orientation. Such a situation is not ripe enough to be in tandem with a high task-orientation. The leader, by keeping cool, must make use of all his traits to make his subordinates understand thoroughly the various aspects of the policy to be implemented, should make them adopt more of a humane attitude vis-a-vis the clients and not referring to rules and procedures everytime and thus letting them drift away from the administration's credibility among the people. He should also endeavour to meet and discuss with a good number of citizens and motivate them to actively extend their co-operation to the administration. All this needs to be done in the most humanistic and friendly way quite apart from the uppish behaviour of the administrators. It is worth highlighting that unless the functionaries are fully well aware of the various dimensions of the policy, have a clear understanding of its positive points and extent of benefit to be given to a particular group and groups, and above all, have a concern for the citizens, the administration can never act effectively.

Under situations where the leader in an administrative organisation feels handicapped on some counts (for example, the subordinates are not co-operative and are not willing to take up any responsibility, and citizens are making excessive demands and obstructing the way of functioning) and the administrator, after understanding all the related facets, draws the inference that the subordinates and citizens have a low level of maturity, he should adopt the 'Selling Style' of leadership which involves high task and high relationship behaviour. Functionaries who are unable but willing to take responsibility are confident but lack skill at the same time. Thus what is required on the part of administrative leader is to adopt a selling style which provides not only directive behaviour, because of the lack of ability of the subordinates, but also supportive behaviour for reinforcing their willingness and enthusiasm, which is required to deal with functionaries with a low maturity level.

In situations where the administrator as a leader of his team and organisation feels that his subordinates are able but unwilling to do what is assigned to them, the functionaries have lack of confidence and feel insecure with one thing or the other and this affects their performance, the leader should adhere to the 'Participating Style' of leadership and share with the subordinates decision making pertaining to important issues relating to the working of his organisation. The leader is to play the role of a facilitator and a communicator. It would involve high relationship and low task behaviour on the part of the leader. It is somewhat close to the 'Developer Style' of leadership mentioned earlier.

The administration, especially at the lower levels, comes in contact with the citizens and politicians to a considerable extent. In a situation where the citizens are more and more demanding and politicians are pressing the administration hard for having benefits accorded to their selective favourites, the leader must adopt a style suitable to the situation. He should be a developer in making the citizens understand

and should also be a benevolent autocrat with the functionaries for getting the targets attained. He should simultaneously be tactful in dealing with the politicians for achieving his purpose in the best interest of his organisation and clientele with the least resentment from the majority.

The role and responsibility of the leadership is of great magnitude, importance and significance in an administration. By virtue of personal traits, position, authority, and status the leader can do wonders in moulding the work performance of his organisation in accordance with the needs, desires, wants, expectations and aspirations of all concerned--citizens, subordinates, seniors, and politicians. The leader's role can be of great significance in creating responsiveness on the part of the administration.

Decision Making

A large number of decisions, with regard to day-to-day work of routine and non-routine nature are being taken everyday in the administrative organisations operating at lower or upper levels of administration. Though so many decisions are taken in every office, yet a good section of the clientele of each office is not satisfied with the administrative decisions taken. It is holding truth to say that the majority of the decisions are taken wrongly or to say that the quantum of the public demands has increased so much that the decisions made are unable to serve the large section of the concerned component of the society would not be wrong. Whatever may the case be, it certainly affects the image of the administration, and people who do not get either their cases decided or have them decided wrongly are not satisfied with the process of decision making in the administration and are thus made to believe that the administration is not active and involved so far as the citizens at large are concerned.

What is a decision? A decision is to decide what is to be done for dealing with a specific situation at hand. The action is to be selected from various alternatives before a person taking a decision. Obviously, when it comes to select one out of many alternatives available, the decision maker would attempt to go in for the one which could result in a better output in comparison to the other available alternatives. The success is attempted to be maximised and failures minimised while choosing the favoured alternative.

The famous decision theorist, Herbert A. Simon has analysed the process of decision-making in three stages.[13] The first phase has been termed by him as 'Intelligence Activity'. In it the environment is searched for conditions calling for decision-making or it could be said that after a thorough probe and analysis the problems being confronted by the organisation are identified for the purpose of taking up the efforts to sort out the problems and meet the challenges at hand.

The second phase is called 'Design Activity'. In it the problems identified are viewed at length and conscientious efforts are made to develop various possible alternatives to meet the situation. It is also a phase of much importance because the problems have to be analysed at length and all possible alternatives or courses of action need to be designed with all possible pros and cons of each alternative.

Simon has termed the third phase as 'Choice Activity'. In it all the pros and cons of each alternative designed in the preceding phase are taken serious note of and finally the best alternative out of the available ones is selected. Decisions are made often to aim at maximum and optimal results. The decision makers will make use of either the statistical data and empirical evidence, or a clear-cut logic of their own while making the decision.

Like any other organisation, as mentioned earlier, the administrative organisation also has a number of problems and aspects to be sorted out by making decisions. An administrative organisation takes basic as well as routine decisions. The routine decisions are the ones which are of repetitive nature and have little impact on the overall work mechanism of an organisation but affect the clientele of the administrative organisation. Supposing dealing with issue 'A' of individual 'K' the administrative agency decided in accordance with alternative 'Y' and dealing with issue 'A' of individual 'M' the alternative selected by the same or similar agency is instead alternative 'Z', the confusion could be apparent. For dealing with such routine cases, the administration needs to adopt a uniform policy. Basic decisions are quite unlike routine decisions as these are not of repetitive nature but are unique by themselves. Supposing a new policy having been formulated has been passed on to the administrative agency for implementation and is of a different nature compared to the earlier policies implemented, in such a case a comptele planning regarding the restructuring of the organisation and making sub-organisations at various levels, allocation of resources, etc., is to be formulated. As the work to be undertaken would not be similar to that done earlier, the organisation has to seriously think over various related facets for dealing with the situation effectively.

Other types of decisions in the administration are organisational and personal. There is scope for delegation to others in some cases so far as the organisational decisions are concerned but the personal decisions are the ones which cannot be delegated. It is not that easy to make a distinction between the organisational decisions aimed at the attainment of organisational goals and personal decisions of the administrators aimed at the achievement of personal goals. Administrator 'A' wants to prove his administrative acumen while working in a rural development wing. Would he not aim at the success of the wing under his charge? At times the personal decisions smoothen the organisational decisions and vice-versa.

It is often said that the decisions made in the administration are irrational and lopsided and protect the interests of one and not of others. The 'element of rationality' in a decision is the one which is based on appropriate means used to arrive at the decision. Dealing with human beings and their problems which are dynamic in nature, it is very difficult to justify or cope with the means and ends approach in administrative decision. A look at the working of administrative systems would reveal that an administration is so over-burdened alongwith its other constraints that to develop most appropriate means to achieve an end is very difficult. Furthermore, the element of the superior's control over the juniors would always be an important ingredient in the decision made in the organisation. In such cases would it not be the personal rationality of the boss, even if he attempts to decide the appropriate means for achieving the end? It is possible that the boss has limited knowledge about the problem being tackled by him and he makes use of his limited experience or knowledge to design means. It would bc, in such cases, a subjective and not objective rationality.

Keeping in view the complexities and dynamism in which the administrative organisations operate, these agencies should never adopt the approach of passing-on-the-buck in the court of the leader of the organisation for deciding or taking the decision. It should be made a participative effort of all concerned. A thorough and consistent system of identifying problems being confronted by the administrative organisation should be evolved. The persons having the responsibility to decide about the various related facets of the organisation should be completely aware of all possible alternatives and they should make detailed analysis of various alternatives designed. Even at the stage of selection of an alternative, efforts should be to have the selection based on detailed discussions among the decision-making group members having absolute freedom to express their point of view.

Normally, there are three different situations in general in which the capability of the administration's decision-making is seen through. All these situations need to be handled very tactfully so that the work is performed in such a manner that a sizeable section of the clientele feels satisfied about the functioning of the administrative channels. It has been observed that a majority of the cases pertaining to the citizens demands, needs, and expectations are the ones which do not need any long exercise to be taken for making decisions. In other words, a good number of decisions pertaining to these cases are routine decisions to be made under conditions of certainty. Under such situations decision makers are aware of the different alternatives and have to select the one out of the many which has a potential for maximum benefits to the maximum number of affected persons, of course, within the framework of rules, regulations and as per procedures, with minimum loss to minimum people, and with minimal resources in terms of manpower, time, and finances. With regard to the production in public industrial organisations or developmental aimed sectors of production, the maximum could be determined by putting to use techniques like mathematical programming. Under conditions of certainty the decision maker is aware of and can assess the probabilities associated with the outcomes of the alternative/alternatives selected as decision/s in different situations.

The situations where it becomes difficult for the decision maker in the administration to assess the probabilities which could be associated with the outcomes are tricky because of the uncertainty. These situations require to be taken care of in a more serious manner because in such cases the administration may not be fully in the know of the absence of any basis for a clear appraisal of various alternatives and thus may attempt to justify its own selection as the best in one way or the other.

An example of a practical situation of making decisions under conditions of uncertainty by the administration could be handling a students' strike and maintaining law and order by ordering shooting. With no or little awareness of the probabilities, the decision maker may emphasise more on such aspects which he believes did contribute in making him decide the way he did. It would get him a sense of relief and he would feel encouraged to know that he had decided on the basis of rationality. But suppossing the order was for shooting and a good number of persons died as a result of it. The outcomes are very serious. Would the administrator under such circumstances be able to justify his stand merely wielding his cards of rationality. Or, if he does not order shooting and the situation further worsens then what would be the outcome. In conditions of uncertainty the probabilities for each of the two said alternatives are not known to the administrator. Whatever was his decision was on the basis of specific criteria which represented assumptions with regard to the circumstances from which he proceeded in the said selected way. His criteria of selecting the alternative could have been based either on conservatism or optimism. There is very little scope for making use of quantitative techniques for making decisions in situations which are not certain. One technique which could be made use of in such situations is that the administrator endeavours to calculate for himself the worst possible outcomes which possibly could take place with regard to all available alternatives and then an alternative is selected which has the least negativities possibly attached with it. It is known as 'Minimax technique' of decision-making. Another technique which could be used in uncertain situations is known as 'Bayes procedure'. In it the decision maker attempts to utilise the expected values concept and each outcome which possibly could take place is assumed as having equal chance of occurring.

The third situation is the situation of Risks. These situations fall in between the certain and uncertain situations. In such situations the decision maker is in the know of the probabilities of each alternative and he must be concerned about the various possible outcomes. He is able to make himself aware of the probabilities of the alternatives on the basis of past happenings of a similar kind with regard to different/all probable alternatives. The element of risk whisks in with a particular happening taking place with regard to any alternative's any outcome though the same did not take place earlier. "This a priori evidence serves as the basis for selection by the decision maker, a process that tends presumable, towards a maximization of gains. Actual decision-making, however, does not proceed as clearly and as easily as might be indicated. As with uncertainty, the many statistical and behavioural concomitants make the choice in risky situations extremely variable".[14]

It is difficult to make decision in risky situations because the decision maker has a limited knowledge, information and experience with regard to the probabilities of the alternatives and also there are many outcomes possible for each alternative. There are two types of probabilities which have the possibility to be applied to decisions in risky situations. Firstly, the objective statistical probability which enables the decision maker to put to use the mathematical calculations for calculating possible outcomes and drawing inferences. Under this technique the decision maker attaches fifty per cent chance to the outcome to be fruitful and the remaining as unsuccess chances. The probability is to be determined by computing all the probabilities out of the 100 per cent in the fray to make sure of what the immediate next one would be. The chances could be to get an outcome contrary to the one thought of. Such limitations are and would be there in making use of this technique but if it is properly applied and interpreted and quantitative technique is appropriately made use of, the chances for it to be an effective tool are many in comparison to the subjective probability, the other technique to take decisions in risky situations. This technique does not have any mathematical computation or calculation and is based on guesses or speculations of the decision maker. The administrator endeavours to decide by thinking in his own mind about various probabilities of the alternatives. Compared to objective statistical probability, this technique has more risks and dangers involved in it.

It is the dream of probably all the heads of the organisations that their subordinates should work with utmost enthusiasm and zeal and the targets and goals of the organisation should be achieved if not in the minimum possible time at least in the stipulated time. It holds truc of the heads of administrative agencies too. They also strive for developing a feeling and sense of participation among their subordinates. But such efforts at developing a sense of participation do not result in expected outcomes because the subordinates are seldom involved in making decisions in accordance with which they are to work. The administrators attempt to carry their subordinates alongwith them but rarely make efforts to have their involvement in the decision-making process. It is a fact that some amount of time would be consumed in getting participative decisions made but the net result would be of greater quality in terms of time and other related inputs. It would inculcate among the subordinates a feeling that they are having responsibility with regard to the functioning of their organisation.

Properly devised mechanism, on the part of seniors in the administrative organisations at distinct and various levels of administration, for making decisions in such a manner that it is conducive to the situation and the optimal results could be attained, has to be evolved. The efforts of the powers to be reckoned with in making the total process simple and participative, in line with the dynamism involved in it, would go a long way in making an administrative organisation not only attain its goals but also do it in a manner which contributes in improving the image of the administration in the eyes of the citizens. The functionaries would be in a position to carry out the work in a fair and impartial manner promptly and effectively. It would lead to making the administration responsive to the society and the system as such.

Job Design

It cannot be expected of a functionary to provide his maximum effort for the attainment of goals assigned to him unless he or she draws satisfaction from the job supposed to be performed by him or her. It is normally felt that hardly any attention is paid to know whether the functionaries have job satisfaction or not and seldom measures are adopted to get them such jobs which are designed to attain the maximum productivity through making them satisfied with their assigned jobs. On the basis of a research survey, four measures of a general job satisfaction were determined as (i) pride in work group, (ii) intrinsic job satisfaction, (iii) organisation's involvement; and (iv) financial and job status satisfaction.[15] Unless efforts are made in the administrative channels to seriously think of making people perform the jobs suitable to their interests, optimal performance can never be achieved. Normally what happens in government organisations is that an individual at the start of his service is assigned a particular task which he is to perform for a fairly long time. No concern is attached to find out whether that person is interested in taking up that kind of job or not. Furthermore, without any major involvement of finances or other resources the routine and so called monotonous jobs can even be designed as interesting ones but no effort is made in this direction. Once the public offices start designing the jobs appropriately the positive effects on work done by the functionaries would be great and good a number of obstructions in the way of making administration responsive would be removed.

Fredrick Herzberg and associates had, on the basis of their research, drawn the inference that presence of factors like, achievement, recognition, work itself, responsibility, advancement and growth in a job play a substantive role in motivating the employees to work hard for the attainment of the goals of the organisation. A close look at these factors would reveal that for ensuring the possibility of these vis-a-vis the jobs to be performed by the functionaries would not cost anything to the organisation and, therefore, qualitative and quantitative output could be looked for. Alongwith the said factors having been termed as 'Motivators' resulting in a high state of motivation, the other factors termed as 'Hygiene Factors' have been identified by these scholars as pay, supervision, organisation's policies, co-worker relationship, etc. The state of motivation among the functionaries in an office would simply not arrive by putting into use the hygiene factors because it would bring them only to the neutral state of motivation to be converted into a high state of motivation only through motivating factors. By ushering in basic changes in the nature of the job to be performed by employees, their motivation can be enhanced. Jobs need to be designed in a manner that the functionaries get not only challenge and responsibility by performing the same but also recognition, advancement, and growth. The point can be contested so far as the public offices are concerned on the count that in government organisations there is hardly any discretion or scope with the top administration to pave way for advancement and growth of good working functionaries through promotion. But the scope could always be made for motivating the people by recognising their efforts through letters of appreciation, commendation certificates and wherever possible to help in promoting the insider hard workers. Responsibility could be passed on to them for various tasks making their jobs and functioning challenging. Moreover, the dissatisfying or the hygiene factors could be taken care of for bringing the employees motivation state to neutral from a low end by providing an impartial and judicious supervision which as far as possible should be of a democratic rather than an authoritative nature, and making the day-to-day governing policies of the organisation sound and encouraging. By inculcating the spirit of oneness and belonging among the employees the relationship of one with other could be made cordial. All these factors would go a long way in making the employees satisfied with their jobs.

Jobs should be designed in such a way that employees do feel the jobs as having characteristics of a variety of tasks to be performed, workable autonomy for undertaking the tasks assigned to the employees, and having scope for using their acquired or inherited knowledge and skills for performing the jobs.[16] Such designed jobs would enable the employees to have enriched jobs and it would not only satisfy them but would also motivate them to perform better. From this it could be inferred that different employees working in various organisations at different places for accomplishing the same or similar kind of work would be using their own knowledge and skills for performing similarly. But this point could be taken care of by making broad guidelines for accomplishing the task, thus leaving the scope with the functionaries to apply their work skills and knowledge for performing it.

High performance of the employees alongwith low output stoppages could be seen through the application of job design principles by taking into account the psychological requirements and necessities of the tasks. The jobs should be designed to have a reasonably demanding content so that these provide learning opportunities to the employees. Coupled with traits of tasks, viz, challenge, autonomy, recognition, the demanding content of the task with opportunities to learn on the part of employees through performing it would make them undertake the tasks in a qualitative and quantitative manner.

Besides the variety of skills required a work, the jobs should be so designed as having task identity and task significance. By task identity is meant the degree to which the job requires completion of a whole and identifiable piece of work that is doing a job from beginning to end with a visible outcome. Task significance implies the degree to which the job has a substantial impact on the lives or work of other people, whether in the same organisation or in the external environment. Not only the jobs should be designed to have task significance but in administration the functionaries should be prepared and developed to appreciate the impact of their tasks' performance on the lives of a considerable number of citizens on the one hand and the administrative system on the other. The net resultant of the jobs designed to include skill variety, task identity, task significance, autonomy, and feedback would be high internal work motivation of the employees, high quality of work performance, high satisfaction with the work, and low absenteeism.

Proper care and attention in analysing the activities to be performed and the way to do so by the top echelons of administration in consultation with the concerned subordinates would pave the way to appropriately table forth various improvements which possibly could be added in the jobs to be performed. Thorough designing of jobs would mean effective and efficient functioning. This would help the administration in becoming responsive to the needs and genuine demands of the citizens, society, and the system.

Goal Setting

Every organisation, whether public or private, strives to attain the goals in an optimal time frame. In fact, it is the goals for the positive attainment of which the procedures are evolved and the division of work done in a way where every functionary is allotted some specific tasks to perform. The employees' motivation and their performance are affected by the role played by goals and the way the goals are fixed in the organisation.

As stated earlier, a goal is such a condition or end which an employee, group of employees, and the organisation as a whole desire to achieve. Goals provide a focus for policy-making and organisational decisions of related types. Clear goals encourage a consistency in administration, planning, and decision-making. Goals exist in the thinking of the administration without being made explicit. Every administrative organisation certainly has some goals which are responsible for its being in existence and which keep it in operation. Goals can be conceptualised as future states of desired affairs. It means the goals are statements of where the organisation wants to be at some future time.[17] It has also been said that goals can be seen as constraints placed on present and future behaviour as a result of past and present decisions and commitments.[18] Both these versions have been treated as distinct from each other,[19] but it is not exactly so. Both are rather complementary to each other. In the light of the present limitations, constraints and hope for better conditions, the organisations fix their future goals.

The administrative organisations also have goals to be achieved in a purposeful manner. It is unfortunate that in a majority of organisations there is lack of clarity about the goals and also about the time frame for meeting them. As a result, the goals which guide and direct the behaviour of the employees by focusing their attention in specific directions are unable to do so. It is also true in the administrative set-up that goals which often serve as a standard against which judgement can be made as to the relative effectiveness and efficiency with which individuals achieve their purposes are unable to serve the desired purpose. Because of lack of a clear picture before the employees in the shape of goals to be pursued the employees are not in a position to contribute their best to their organisations. On the other end, there are a number of administrative organisations in which there is absolute clarity of goals and the time framework. In most of these organisations also the goals are not accomplished in time and in the required best manner. The reason in such cases is the wrong fixation of goals. Attempts, as often seen in administration, are made to achieve what is humanly not possible in a specified period of time. Difficult and challenging goals are more rewarding and preferred to the easy and mundane goals but for achieving them two pre-requisites are a must. First, the true motivated work force having a commitment and sense of belonging to the work and the system, and secondly, the required infra-structure for the attainment of difficult goals. Somehow or the other, the functionaries involved in governmental administration feel neither that much motivated nor committed to their respective organisations. Furthermore, there is always some inadequacy with regard to the required infrastructural resources. Under such conditions to expect something like accomplishing difficult and challenging goals would be a sheer mistake. It is here where the true administrative acumen of the administrative leaders stands to be tested. They can play a substantive role in not only motivating their subordinates but also in fixing up the goals to be achieved in such a way that an employee's conscious intention is touched upon and the goals regulate his actions. The goals should be so fixed that the employees attempt to achieve it. "It is not enough to know that an order or request was made: one has to identify whether or not the individual heard it and understood it, how he appraised it, and what he decided to do about it before its effects on his behaviour can be predicted and explained.[20]

It is often witnessed in administration that the goals fixed are not specific and to the point but are vague or general. It does not leave any scope with the functionaries to fix a frame of time for themselves to accomplish the targets supposed to be covered by them. Making an employee know for sure what is expected of him is always to be preferred to fixing his goals of work as "try as hard as you can" or "try to do better than last year" or "do your best". Such kinds of idealistic phrases are not going to help in the attainment of the targets in a meaningful way. Attached closely to it is the point that goals should be fixed in a specified way through participation of the employees for whom the goals are being fixed. Every individual would try to do his best for the task in which he had been involved at its very start. Imposed orders for performing a particular task could be adhered to but certainly with not all the zeal and enthusiasm of the performer. A goal fixed through discussion with and participation of the employees would be termed by them as an accepted and owned goal which would definitely mean more commitment of theirs in comparison to an assigned goal. Another point of utility through participatory fixation of goals could be that the employees would get an opportunity to not only put forth but also get a way to their values, value judgements, emotions and desires to the goals to be fixed. All this would have a substantive impact on their behaviour towards work to be performed.

Timely feedback based on objective assessment and facts always help the performer improve his functioning. While fixing the goals, in the total mechanism, enough scope should be made whereby the employees assigned the tasks get feedback about their performance. Unfortunately such a system is not found in the administrative functioning. At times no feedback is given and where it is given it is not objective. Subjective assessment and feedback could be too negative a factor. Even where timely and objective feedback is given the same is not taken in the right spirit by the concerned employee. All this reveals a complete mistrust and lack of faith in the minds of the administrative functionaries. These factors put together very badly affect the working of the administrative organisations ultimately adversely affecting the work output both in quality and quantity. This affects the citizens, society and the system. The responsiveness of administration could be increased by fixing proper goals at proper times.

Delegation of Authority

In simple words it means the assignment of decision-making responsibility to subordinate officials. It is essential that heads of large organisations in the administration delegate some of their authority to the others for a better accomplishment of the tasks and moreover for leaving enough time with the superiors to seriously ponder over other important issues relating to the working of their organisations. Delegating the authority to subordinates would not only reduce the work load of the superiors giving them time and opportunity to take care of other important things but would result in prompt disposal of cases at the lowest levels and satisfying the client group and also the performers by making them responsible. But a number of points and issues are attached with this simple looking aspect. Firstly, what and how much should be delegated? Secondly, are the functionaries who are delegated the authority capable and willing to accept it?; and thirdly, is the superior who is to delegate ready to delegate his authority?

It is in the prime interest of the organisation that the authority should be delegated to such levels where it is required. An illustration could be that a decision has been made in accordance with which the cases of similar type are to be decided. Under such situations the administration functionaries at the lower levels should be delegated the authority to do so and such issues should not unnecessarily be referred to the highest authority for decision. As far as possible the authority should be delegated in almost all such matters/issues which are of routine nature. This would encourage the subordinates, facilitate work performance, and give a chance to superiors to attend to exceptional cases. But it does not mean that authority should be delegated only in cases of routine nature. In some of the exceptional cases as well where the head of the organisation is convinced about the ability of the subordinates the authority could be delegated. The second point of concern is whether the functionaries who are delegated the authority are capable and willing to accept the responsibility. It is a fact that through delegation the work would be performed effectively and efficiently besides activating the functionaries. But it could be dangerous if the authority is delegated to such functionaries who are either not capable or are not willing to accept the same. In such cases instead of looking for better results the outcome could be quite negative. The delegating authority must ensure that the functionary to whom he is delegating is not only capable to deal with it but also has enough motivation to do that. The important question which follows is: who is capable and who is willing? The capability of the subordinate could be adjudged on his past performance record and his inclination to do the work could be adjudged by talking to him. It could be attempted to inculcate a feeling of willingness in a capable but unwilling mind by involving him in the process of fixing the goals and then delegating the authority. The biggest problem which stands in the way of delegating authority is the delegator himself in case of administrative organisations. Unless and until not only the delegator is willing to delegate but is also keen on making the delegation effective it is not possible to have positive effect. In most of the cases, it is observed that the superior has utmost love for the authority he has. He wants to perform all the things under his charge himself without having it being performed by others. In Indian administrators this feeling of possessiveness of their authority makes them unable to accept a situation where their own authority is being used by their subordinates. It not only affects the working but also stands in the way of seniors devoting more time to exceptional or non-routine matters.

At times the heads of the administrative organisations do not delegate their authority because of the fear that doing so would expose them and bring to light the administrative shortcomings which were being practised earlier. In cases where the superiors are weak, have complexes, have poor procedures of work, and wrong methods in practice, the officers do not delegate authority.

To undertake a particular task 'A' in a given amount of time the authority to perform the task could be delegated by the superior to the subordinate but it does not mean that the superior would not be responsible for the outcome of that task. He would still be held responsible in case anything wrong or unwanted is done with regard to it. Because of being overall responsible, the superiors do not delegate their authority. Probably they forget on such occasions that it is their office obligations which are to be performed and are in the interest of or in line with the organisational goals and objectives. They must be ready to take up the required risk of passing the buck to others for the attainment of the stipulated targets promptly. Besides, they must have faith in their subordinates and should be able to make them responsible enough to handle the tasks effectively and efficiently. Furthermore, where is the assurance that nothing would go wrong when undertaken by the superiors themselves. Rather the chances for such a situation appear to be more when the authority is not delegated by the superiors.

It is also felt that somehow or the other the superiors in administrative organisations believe that they are the only capabale and judicious persons to perform the things and their subordinates are lazy, ineffective, incapable and unwilling to do the same. This kind of feeling is responsible for the superiors not delegating their authority and keeping all the things in their own performance schedule. It is an absolutely baseless feeling as no single person is capable and intelligent enough to perform each and everything all by himself. Instead of forcefully strengthening this uncalled for feeling, the superiors should rather endeavour to inculcate a sense of confidence in the subordinates for performing the tasks through delegated authority in the best manner. It has also been observed that the superiors'do adhere to the feeling that their subordinates' don't require authority for performing an assigned task. They feel that the subordinates can do the same as expected without any authority having been delegated to them. Such perception of subordinates feelings or underestimation of the work to be performed without authority have a negative effect. The subordinates, contrary to superiors thinking, do not get alongwith the superiors perception. Such a clash in the perceptions does not help but rather stalls the effective functioning of the administrative organisations.

The delegation of authority in administrative organisations cannot be made effective unless the activities to be performed are classified and grouped together for creating sub-organisations or small units in the bigger organisations. Each such sub-unit of the organisation would not only endeavour to attain its own objectives but would also contribute to the attainment of the overall objectives of that organisation. Such types of objectives to be achieved by the sub-units would enable the top level administration to ascertain the type and quantum of authority required to be delegated. Once ascertained, the administration could go ahead with evolving the mechanism for developing the personnel to not only willingly accept the authority but also accomplish the tasks for which the authority is being delegated. Hence, the greater need for the delegant to assure his ability to perform the assigned tasks. It also becomes obligatory on the part of the delegator to provide the required help and resources alongwith the authority. Authority and responsibility need to go together. Simple delegation of authority to a subordinate without making him responsible for the work for which the authority has been delegated would be a lopsided effort. On one hand the authority provides to a subordinate the right of taking decision for undertaking the tasks, and on the other, the responsibility makes him to go in for the results obtained in a rightful manner without misusing the authority delegated. The ultimate purpose would not be fulfilled unless the authority delegated has an element of responsibility on the part of delegant goes alongwith it. One thing needs to be made clear here that when the delegator delegates the authority he does not and cannot delegate his responsibility regarding the issue in question to the delegant. No superior official can escape responsibility simply by delegating his authority. In such a situation it becomes more important on the part of the superior to develop his subordinates to whom he is delegating the authority to pursue the assigned task more seriously and meaningfully so that besides its accomplishment in time the delegator does not have to face any odd situation.

In administrative organisations the delegation of authority could be of great utility provided adequate and required authority is delegated to the juniors for making appropriate use of the same through output of the specified tasks both in quality and quantity. Some prerequisites for making delegation of authority effective are:

a) The delegant must be made conscious and aware of the authority delegated to him and also of his responsibility towards the delegator with regard to it. This would enable the subordinate to precisely know what he is expected to do and what authority he has to accomplish the task. It would result in prevention of overlapping of authority and would also do away with the gaps between authority and responsibility;

b) For getting the maximum out of the use of the principles of delegation of authority, a conducive work environment has to be made in the organisation. The subordinates to whom the authority has been delegated must be treated with special care. Besides proper monitoring, objective and timely feedback, the superiors must attempt to provide a chance of improving in case the delegant makes some mistake in his work. He should be given an opportunity to learn from his experience and the experience of the delegator;

c) Before delegating the authority, the top administrator in the organisation must very seriously work on the total issue. He must jot down clearly the goals and the time frame for achieving the same. The second aspect is to select the subordinates within the organisation, of course, keeping in view the structure and infrastructure of the organisation and the selected ones must be prepared and developed to accept the authority before it is delegated to them for the attainment of the specified targets. Attempts must be made to fix the goals for every chosen delegant in consultation with him so that he does not take the assigned responsibility and delegated authority as an imposed one;

d) Every care should be taken by the delegator in chosing the delegants. In accordance with the demands of the tasks, the delegants having positive interest and inclination for the same must be selected. The personal traits of the employee and the requirements of the task assigned to him must have a close match because a mismatch in these two would be having quite negative an impact on the work output. After making the choice of the delegants, proper and required training should be imparted to them for the accomplishment of the assigned tasks. Unfortunately, least care is attached to it in administrative organisations in India. It is believed that an employee in an organisation is fit to perform any task assigned to him. This is only a myth and so should be properly dealt with; and

e) Normally in governmental administrative organisations there is only one channel of communication and that is from top downward. Subordinates do strongly feel that seldom they get a chance to communicate openly and freely with the superiors. This would hamper the total aspect of delegation of authority in case the delegant does not have an open channel of communication with the delegator. In fact, both of them are responsible for the given task and both must have open channels of communication for getting the work through.

By making considerate, thorough, and effective use of the principle of delegation of authority, the administrative organisations can attain wonderful tasks in the optimal way in minimal time. Such performance would not only curtail the delay in sorting out and solving the problems of the citizens, but will help in reducing the number of complaints and grievances of the public. Besides, it would clearly help the administration to bring to light its concern for the society and the system.

Decentralisation

It is an administrative concept applied by large administrative organisations in assigning decision-making responsibility to sub-units. It usually takes the form of field-service operations or division of tasks. Decentralisation has been considered to be of great help in getting the tasks performed not only quantitatively but also qualitatively. Contrary to centralisation which has taken the connotation of being conservative and autocratic in nature, ''decentralisation has become the golden calf of management philosophy. It has been lauded by such terms as 'more democratic', 'a step toward world peace', 'greater freedom of spirit and less authoritarian'. The implicit assumption is that centralisation reflects the opposite of these worthy qualities''.[21] Administrative agencies having widely spread over and dealing with the day-to-day as well as non-programmed issues confronting the majority sections of the society cannot afford to be authoritarian, despotic, lethargic, inefficient, and dispirited. Those who occupy the top positions in administrative hierarchies should make every possible attempt to make decentralisation a fact than a fiction. It means that with decentralisation more and more decisions regarding the issues and problems at hand would be taken at the lower levels of the administration. The decisions to be made at the lower levels should not only be more in quantity but should be significant from their importance point of view affecting sizeable number of such functions which possibly need to be taken care of at such levels. In cases where the decisions are made without having much effect and impact on the functions, decentralisation would not be of much importance. Besides this, for making decentralisation more effective such a mechanism needs to be evolved which stresses on less checking to be made on the decisions made at the lower levels. All these points could easily be debated from the other point of view in the sense that more decisions important in nature and affecting a large number of functions at lower levels and with less amount of checking could worsen the situation also. This would be giving more autonomy to the lower levels. Viewing it from the positive end, one finds that a tactful and intelligent way of handling the situations by the superiors in the wake of decentralisation could easily do away with all these so called problems. Followed by it comes the important question with regard to the degree of decentralisation. Should it be maximum, minimum or optimum? Decentralisation should be maximum with regard to the issue, the dealing with which has been made the responsibility of the decentralised authority or agency. Such organisations or sub-organisations within an organisation should be made complete in all respects and by giving them authority to make use of their complete initiative, innonative skills and development of their personnel and units. In such cases there should not be any obstructive tools over them.

A decentralised structure would be suitable to a fast change and a dynamic growth. Keeping in view the quantum of development to take place in almost all fields in countries like India and also the rising expectations and aspirations of the citizens of this independent nation and the system, the administrative structure more so at the lower levels needs to be such as could cope with the speedy changes and growth dynamism. Moreover, decentralisation would mean an effective work performance, project or programme feasibility and awareness which is again most called for in our society and system. Besides, it would be pinpointing the responsibility clearly on the decentralised agencies making them task oriented and seeking for the accomplishment of the same in a specified time frame.[22] The other side of such type of decentralised structure would mean restricting the tendency for innovative tools and growth thereupon of the sub-units concerned only and the difficulty could be there in making allocation of pooled resources among various sub-units. Besides, the problems could be there on account of co-ordinating and integrating common or shared functions.[23] But all these so termed weaknesses of the decentralised structures could be turned into the strengths of decentralised structure by an intelligent handling. Decentralisation implies dynamism and growth to be ushered in by the organisations and sub-organisations who have been focused upon for passing some responsibility on to them through decentralisation. Obviously, the innovations and initiative having been made by them could be taken as trend setting and precedents to be followed and adopted by other organisations and agencies. Even the pooled resources could be made optimal use of by properly planning the way for dealing with the work.

Decentralisation of activities among thoughtfully and carefully chosen organisations or sub-units would prove to be of great significance for the top echelons of administration by not devoting all of their time to the operational decisions but getting time for thinking for the development, growth and operating mechanism for future. Every target group and area has characteristics different from other target groups and areas. Centralised rules and procedures do not allow things to move. Decentralisation would enable the dealing agencies at lower levels to evolve their own mechanism for dealing with problems and citizens depending upon local requirements but all within the broad framework of rules and procedures evolved for the whole state, division or district. Decentralisation gives work freedom to the lower structure. The personnel involved therein would certainly feel motivated by the authority and responsibility passed on to them. It would also enable them to chalk out their own line of action to be adopted for accomplishing the particular task. Hence, they can join their heads and hands together for fixing up their goals within the overall targets of the government to that effect. This feeling of importance would mean a lot for the work force. Besides motivation, it would go a long way in providing opportunities to the employees at lower level or in a decentralised structure to learn more and more from their experiences. It would mean encouragement to the employees to develop themselves for the attainment of the targets passed on to their folds. The delays in administrative work would also be curbed because the issues could be decided at the lower levels and would not often be sent to the higher levels for clearance or decision on each and everything. The levels of operations would be minimised again reducing the time in deciding a particular issue.

Through decentralisation, self-sufficient units would come in existence meaning thereby reduction in the number of levels involved. By way of decentralising the tasks to be performed by different sub-units in an organisational structure the problems for co-ordinating the various important activities related to a specific task assigned to a sub-unit at the operational level would be minimised. The references to be made or information to be sought could be dealt with at that level only without being passed on to the other sub-units. Though the sub-units can never be completely independent all by themselves, yet it would mean a lot when the specific sub-units have been allotted a task with freedom to perform it.

As mentioned earlier, decentralisation in administrative organisations is more of a fiction than a fact. The administrators talk about it without meaning it. Likewise, the lower echelons want to have decentralisation from the top but without properly understanding what it is and how it is to be made use of. For decentralisation to be made effective, primarily the concept of decentralisation needs to be thoroughly understood by all concerned. Decentralisation means that the incumbents would be made independent to perform a specifically assigned task and to take decisions for the same in the light of the broad policy-responsibility continuum. It does not mean that the incumbents have been given absolute autonomy and they can do things the way they like. It cerainly does imply that an environment has to be made wherein the subordinates develop the feeling of independence for acting with courage to take right decisions in accordance with the situation and tasks.

For making operations and responsibilities decentralised there has to be a centralised control in order to integrate different sub-units getting authority and responsibility to work in line with the broad policy and its objectives. Under the garb of such centralisation at the top, it should not be misutilised and misinterpreted, rather it should have its limits confined only to certain basic activities which are felt to be necessary for making decentralisation effective.

It is a fact that with decentralisation the number of sub units would come to the fore having the responsibility of attaining some predetermined objectives. In order to see that these units are doing justice to the tasks assigned certain control techniques for ensuring timely action, speedy performance, benefit to the deserving etc., have to be put to use. It would not be against the spirit of decentralisation but would rather make the decentralised units move in a rightful direction. Through such techniques of control not only the performance of the sub-units vis-a-vis the major targets could be measured but the performance of the individuals involved in the process could also be judged and wherever required changes or feedback for improvement could be given.

For making the various sub-units having been assigned the status of decentralised ones work in a proper and effective way it becomes obligatory on the part of the top administration to appropriately develop the so called heads or those in charge of the sub-units and through them the other functionaries for the tasks to be performed. Through decentralisation a challenge would be thrown open to the functionaries and they have to be prepared for doing justice to the assigned tasks. The total process should not be launched in a haste. It should be put into use only after making all involved thoroughly prepared and developed and to begin with its pace should be relatively slow so that employees could get alongwith it in the overall interest of the organisation and in turn its objectives and goals.

Through decentralisation the lower echelons of administration would be given the responsibility and duty for undertaking the tasks for which these levels are approached. With proper authority at their command these sub-organisations could take a decision on the issues affecting the public which are under their performance zone. This would not only help in attaining the targets but would mean prompt action on the demands, needs and grievances of the public relating to it. It would help in making the administration act more responsibly and responsively.

Communication

The administrative system of our country is thoroughly vast and widespread. From the union capital to a remote village there are a number of channels, agencies and organisations in existence. The prime task of all these is to deliver goods to the public in the light of various governmental policies, usher in development in chosen sectors, and maintain a regulatory administration. Broad policies are formulated at top levels and the same percolate down to the lower levels for its execution. Vast number of employees serving the governmental administrative system are involved in this process. Whatever is to be done and the way it is to be done is passed on from the top to the bottom through various modes of communication. It is the basic process of communication through which everything between the top to the lower echelons is passed on or conveyed. It is often used in the sense of transmitting information mainly through writing in the governmental sectors. Communication plays an important role not only in the overall functioning of the governmental system but it also reflects the image of the government and shows its effect and impact on the society and the system. Supposing a policy 'K' has been formulated at the state level. It will pass through the Secretariat, Directorate, Division, District and then to the Sub-Division or Block levels. Any mistake done anywhere in the long process would prove to be thoroughly fatal by the time the communication would reach the concerned executing agency. Normally, there is one-way communication in the administrative system. This means the transmission of message from the sending channel to the receiving channel without having any provision for response from the receiving end as to whether the message has been properly received and understood. Consequent upon it, much is left to the imaginative interpretation of the communication received by the receiving channel. At times this amounts to utter distortion of the basic sense of the message transmitted. This type of communication is not required and it affects the working of the administration to a substantial extent. Ample chances of delays, misinterpretation, wrong execution, and the like are some aspects which could surface upon as a result of it. Basically communication has to be "the flow of material, information, perception and understanding between various parts and members of the organisation... all methods, means and media of communication (communication technology), all the channels, networks and systems of communication (organisational structure), and all the person-to-person interchange (interpersonal communication) needs to be made use of".[24]

In the administrative organisation much depends on the way the things to be executed are communicated and properly understood by the executing channels. Little lack of clarity can amount to abundant distortions in the overall impact of the policy to be executed. The way the administrative functionaries communicate with the citizens, with other colleagues in the same organisation, with superior levels in the organisation, and with other related government organisations is of great significance for the administrative system. Though the organisational communication is of great importance and has enormous bearing on the execution of a specific scheme, yet the inter-personal communication, that is, the communication between employees and constituents of society apparently appears to have more impact on the public and does reveal the kind and quantum of interest the administration has for the citizens at large.

The message or information to be conveyed could either be oral or written. Oral communication is where the sender and the receiver exchange their ideas through words or expressions face to face or through words either facing each other or through devices like telephone, wireless, etc. Though oral communication is better in the sense that chances of getting the doubts cleared and for having a proper understanding of the issue at hand on the part of the receiver are more, yet in the government administration oral communication is not encouraged much because there is no record of anything through this type of communication. In written communication the message or information is conveyed through words in black and white, graphs, pictures, diagrams, etc. Such communication could always be stored for the purpose of further references to the same. Written communication is also considered to be binding on the subordinates and the superiors could take action against the defaulting employees if the written communication is not adhered to.

Organisational communication is of three types viz: Downward, Upward, and Horizontal. In most of the governmental administrative organisations, there is dominance of the first type of communication, that is, Downward communication, which has a one-way flow from the top to the bottom. Through it the top levels of administration communicate to the lower levels in writing about what is to be done? Which procedures are to be adopted? How it is to be done? In what time is it to be done? What should be the level of the performance of the employees? And, what is expected of them? etc. This is also more in the form of directive from the top to the bottom without leaving enough choice and chance with the receiver to stand and appreciate the basic sense of the number of clauses in the communication passed on to him. Downward communication in the administrative system is treated like a directive that needs to be attended to and cared for as per the time specifications. If all directions are followed, the net result would be a thorough success. But it does not happen. Though employees are supposed to abide by the communication from the top, it is not done in the spirit in which the communication has been issued. Reasons for it could be many. For example, the communication which is not as per the basic beliefs and values of the employees would be resisted by them. Secondly, where there is lack of clarity in even one of the points in the total message the execution gets affected. Thirdly, any communication would be treated as one of the many received every day and not much attention would be given to it. Fourthly, a large number of orders and circulars which again are part of the downward communication would not be properly maintained, because of lack of infrastructural resources, thus affecting their compliance. All these factors speak of the negativities of the downward communication.

But keeping in view the total structure of the administrative system it is required in almost all the cases that the communication is to be initiated from the top. There is no denying the utility of initiation from the top but it should not be the sole form of communication. The channel of communication has to be kept open by the top levels for the lower levels in order to make things clear to them and also to incorporate some valuable points suggested by the lower levels. Before sending a written communication efforts must be made by the top administrators to discuss the same with the seniors at the lower levels. This would lead to greater clarity, understanding, and least resistance to the communication from the top later on. Besides, an environment of the organisation needs to be made in such a way that there is no scope for misinterpreting the directives issued through a downward written communication. Though the overall execution process would be delayed for some time because of the move to involve the actual implementation channels in the setting up of optimal targets and procedures for the same but the results would be comparatively more positive.

The other form of communication is upward communication or subordinate-initiated communication. In a majority of the cases such communication is more of a reporting nature whereby the subordinates inform the superiors about their work performance, work performance of their teams, performance appraisal of their juniors, etc. Besides this, the clarification of a downward communication is also sought. An analysis of such communication does not show any initiative having been shown by the subordinates by way of suggestions for improvements in the working, etc., or how a specific policy could best be executed, or how the cooperation of citizens, politicians, and voluntary organisations could be solicited. The reason for it could be that the overall environment of administrative organisations is so bureaucratic that the 'Top Boss' is hardly ready to receive such a communication from the down channel. Not only this, the subordinates do not find the atmosphere free and participatory. Encouraging upward communication and also considering seriously the points of views coming from below could improve the total system considerably. It could be done if the top levels keep their doors and minds open to receive suggestions from the lower ones and encourage them for the same. Participative decision-making technique could help a lot in putting to effective use the upward communication. These things would not only help in improving the work environ but would also amount to a more faithful adherence to the organisational directives and orders. Besides, it would make employees feel committed having a sense of belonging to the organisation.

The third type of communication in an organisation is the horizontal communication. By it is meant communication among people at the same level of hierarchy. Normally it is found that persons working in the same organisation develop a sort of allergy for good number of their colleagues. Such relationship stands in the way of effective performance of the tasks and a reference made from one functionary to another is not attended to properly. In other words it could be said that one of the most difficult problems that the administrative organisations face pertains to lateral communication, that is, horizontal communication. The best way of improving it again is the better quality of communication, written, oral, discussions, etc. Besides, the feeling of trust amongst each other needs to be developed between them so that one does not attach wrong motives to a reference made by the other. The benefits of effective horizontal communication include coordination of tasks, problem solving, information sharing and resolving of conflicts. Furthermore, it could play an important role in making a healthy work environment and ultimately helping the public to get their issues decided without delays and harassment.

Normally, it is felt that when a citizen approaches an administrative functionary he is not being properly advised and guided about the problems faced by him. The communication which is mostly oral between the official at the desk and the citizen as the client is of a very poor standard. None is ready to disseminate the information, even when it is not a secret, to a common citizen. Besides, no one cares to communicate properly with the citizens. Though it could be argued that the functionaries do not have time to deal properly with each and every person who approaches them and they are also not supposed to leak out the information to the public, yet the other side of the coin could be that the time spent in misbehaving with the person or rejecting his demand straightaway and even curtly could be sufficient enough to deal with him in a proper manner. The same message could also be communicated with courtesy. Moreover, the information which requires to be conveyed to the public should preferably be depicted through charts and diagrams rather than having the same in files under the custody of the employees. A proper mechanism of communicating the message from the top to the bottom with the lower levels of the organisation given the freedom to seek clarifications on the message (which they should be provided with immediately), sound interpersonal relations between subordinates and the boss, subordinates and peers, functionaries and citizens, functionaries and political leaders, etc. would go a long way in making the citizens appreciate the benefits of the mechanism, and the constraints of the administration regarding some policy matter thus making the administration more responsive to the needs and expectations of the public.

Co-ordination

Interaction among individuals working together in large enterprises or administrative units is an outstanding feature of the present day system. It is also unlikely that this process will be curtailed. It cannot be denied that the organisation can operate effectively only if it proceeds under impersonal rules rather than whims of individuals and presumably under specialists in the administration and other skill areas.

For a proper functioning of an administrative unit whereby the goals or objectives are attained and the citizens are not only satisfied that the administration takes stock of the needs and expectations of the people and promptly responds to the same, the administration has to adequately plan, organise, direct, and control all the resources available with it. As stated earlier, the administrative tasks have not only grown in number but have also become more complex and complicated now. This needs division of work and specialists for the performance of specific tasks in the administration. Furthermore, present day's administrative systems are a set of various sub-systems at work under their respective jurisdictions. All these factors and points when viewed seriously make one think whether coordination could be termed as one of the functions of administration as put in 'POSDCORB' or it is to be considered somewhat more pointedly or specifically. Co-ordination as an activity could accurately be stated as an essence of administration rather than only a function as stated in the 'POSDCORB' approach.

Keeping in view the complexities of the tasks and functional specialisation even in the smallest of the small units of administration, co-ordination could be understood as integration or synchronisation of group efforts in these organisations to achieve its objectives both relating to regulatory as well as developmental functions. It is the orderly synchronizing of efforts of the subordinates or various sub-units of an administrative mechanism to provide the proper amount of timing, and quality of execution, so that their unified efforts lead to the stated objectives, namely the common purpose of that unit.[25] Co-ordination is applied on the efforts of a group of functionaries in various sub-units of a given unit and not on the efforts of a single individual. It is a process which is on-going meaning thereby that it is dynamic in nature and not static having emphasis on unity of efforts by fixing time limits and also on the manner of undertaking the performance of activities of different nature and magnitude and integrating performance of an individual with the total process. The major purpose of coordination is to get the objectives achieved and for a meaningful attainment of organisational goals much depends upon the degree of coordination.

Citizens look towards the administration for a sizeable number of activities relating to their day-to-day lives. Any person approaching a given administrative organisation for any task would feel the importance or significance of coordination because invariably the request he has made shall have to be dealt with by a number of channels and sub-systems for a decision on it. Unless there is clarity of rules and roles within the organisation, the work is bound to be delayed. As pointed out earlier, coordination is not only a function of the administration but an essence of the administration and much depends on the quality of coordination which in turn would bring forth the quality of response of the administration to the public as lack of coordination very badly and severely affects the functioning of any administrative unit.

It is a fact that an administration has a hierarchical structure and is controlled. In a controlled administration, through a chain of command different subordinates at work in different sub-units are under the control of a superior whose duty it is to co-ordinate their activities. By virtue of his position, the boss in a unit has the authority to issue directives to his subordinates for performance of the tasks in his unit in an integrated manner. The boss has to be well informed about the activities under his charge, the division of work, the rules, the goals, and the kind of expectations, needs, demands, and complaints of the clientele for exercising his authority in such a way that all the concerned sub-sections perform their allocated tasks in the specified time.[26] The top boss in the administrative unit must possess qualities of an effective leader whereby he could take his group alongwith him. He should try to make the best use of the democratic or participative style of functioning but if needed he could adopt the autocratic or benevolent styles as well for the purpose of making all function properly. In the absence of effective leadership it is not possible to achieve proper coordination.[27] An established technique for having a better coordination is through committees. The head of the unit should form committees having representatives from each such wing as is involved in a given type of tasks. These representatives should frequently meet to take stock of the work and to find out the bottlenecks, if any, in the overall functioning so that solutions could be put forward for better results.

Co-ordination as an activity appears to be somewhat easy and simple but it is probably one of the most difficult aspects and it does affect the overall functioning of an administrative unit where it is not properly put to use. If an administrative unit has eight sub-units and a particular issue submitted to that unit by a citizen is to be dealt with by four of these eight sub-units and because of lack of co-ordination sub-unit three is not abiding by or standing in the way of explanation given by sub-unit two or one, the issue put forth by the citizen would not be decided quickly. Hence, for making the administration efficient and responsive, it is essential to ensure proper coordination in the units of the administration at all levels.

Motivation

Public administration is the one with which every body comes in contact in regard to the most minute thing as well as the biggest possible problem. The government administrative institutions are also manned by none else but human beings. These human beings also hail from the same sections of the society and are part and parcel of the same social, political and economic systems to which the citizens approaching the administrative system belong. It is also true that the job obligations of the administrative functionaries are the ones wherein the functionaries have the responsibility to perform those for the best interests of the masses -- those who approach them and also those who do not, meaning thereby both the direct and the indirect beneficiaries in the system. If one goes a little deep into the total problem of lack of responsiveness of administration, one could find that the administrative system is much to be held responsible for lack of responsiveness on its part. The functionaries are also to be held equally responsible for the same because basically a system is governed by the functionaries. Why the administrative functionaries behave in a way which does not satisfy the clients is an important issue to be taken care of. One of the significant causes could be that the administrative functionaries are not properly motivated to undertake their duties in the required spirit. It is possible that if they are motivated enough they could do better thus satisfying the citizens and reducing the ever increasing gap between the citizens and the administration. It is a fact that nothing concrete or substantial could be expected from a person who is demotivated or who is not being motivated for performing his job well. Motivation helps to answer what is considered a primary and basic question in the sphere of human behaviour, the question 'why' or 'what is it which makes people do things in a better manner'. It is a process of inducing persons to experience the need for certain desired behaviour and for attaining the efficiency of an administrative unit. As a concept it has taken a variety of forms and could be found in innumerable factors -- traditions, values, customs, philosophies and principles of behavioural science. Motivation is a product of anticipated values from an action and the perceived probability that these values will be attained by an action. It has been depicted as a hypothetical cause of behaviour. It is closely related to behaviour of an individual and the negativities on the count would be reflected in his behaviour thus affecting the performance or jeopardising the administrative work resulting in delays and establishing administration's lack of responsiveness to the needs of citizens. It causes goal-oriented behaviour and plays a substantial role in determining the behaviour of the functionaries in administrative systems. Every individual has a bundle of needs which he attempts to fulfil and the administrative functionaries are no exception to it. As every person attempts in every possible way to achieve his need predominating him at a given point of time, so does the functionary in an administration. Unless the said need is fulfilled all efforts are directed towards that. When one need is fulfilled, it is replaced by another need and the cycle goes on. It is true that all needs being thought of by an individual are never accomplished but the ones which are most basic are supposed to be fulfilled which would make an individual work on the lines which could be more productive. Of course, what is a basic need is a relative term. Need 'A' considered to be basic by individual 'X' may be less significant for individual 'Y'. One should also not forget that the human being has the thinking potential and keeping the circumstances and situations in view he can make compromises with the magnitude and extent of the qualities of his needs but he certainly would attempt to get the same fulfilled whenever he would find the chance to do that. Once the needs considered to be prime and basic by individuals are fulfilled, they decidedly behave qualitatively for accomplishing their duty goals and targets. The administrative bosses heading their units must attempt to find out the factors which could motivate their subordinates. An attempt in the direction of putting such factors towards positive execution would help the employees perform with the maximum zeal and enthusiasm in most of the cases. Maslow has presented a sophisticated classification of needs. These needs, viz: physiological, safety, social, esteem, and self-actualization, make individuals behave in a specific manner for the accomplishment of their wants and desires connected with the need(s).[28] Besides basic needs as put through by Maslow in his theory, the individual in a work organisation gets more motivated by factors, like achievement, recognition, responsibility, advancement, and growth. These are the factors which could help him work more dedicatedly. The administrative functionaries being government employees very clearly know that it is very difficult to get any financial benefits from the government so they do not try much for the same and at the same time they are aware of the slow promotion procedure in the system. Hence, what is left to motivate them is the way to recognize the good work done by anyone, making them more responsible by providing them the jobs which are more challenging, etc. Herzberg has put all these factors under the heading of "Motivators" which he termed as "Satisfiers" also. He has talked of another category of factors under the heading "Hygiene" termed as "maintenance"or "dissatisfiers". These are: policies, supervision, salary, job security, interpersonal relationship with subordinates, supervisors, and peers, working conditions, status, etc.[29] The concept of "dissatisfier" surprised those who thought of the items in that category as positive incentives for work. Herzberg reasoned that many people today consider less time, more money, and more security as "rights". If they are not in line with the expectations, they cause dissatisfaction, but if they are in line, they are often taken for granted. In this respect they prevent dissatisfaction but do not induce positive motivation.

William McDougall has attached importance to vivacious or propulsive principles in human behaviour. He held the view that the psychological forces are certainly not to be visualised as mechanical in operation. He opines that human behaviour is motivated on the basis of an instinctive origin. He has defined instinct as "an inherited or innate psycho-physical disposition which determines its possessor to perceive, or pay attention to objects of a certain class, to experience an emotional excitement of a particular quality upon perceiving such an object, and to act in regard to it in a particular manner or at least, to experience an impulse to such an action".[30] For McDougall, all human behaviour had an instinctive origin. It was contended that if it were not for instincts an individual will be inert, like an intricate clock-work with a broken mainspring.

The functionaries in the administration should be motivated by their top bosses and the system in such a way on the basis of factors like, achievement, recognition, advancement, growth, etc., that they consider the job obligations as natural as play or rest and are able to exercise self-direction and self-control in the service of objectives to which they are committed. The maximum intellectual potentialities of the average functionaries should be thoroughly utilized so that they not only accept but seek responsibility because the capacity to exercise a relatively high degree of imagination, ingenuity, and creativity in the solution of problems is not narrowly but widely distributed in the work force.[31]

A motivated employee force is an asset whereas the demotivated lot is a big liability for the system. Motivated functionaries could play a considerable role in not only providing solutions to the problems faced by the citizens but also anticipating the problems and offering ways to deal with the same before being put forth as problems by the citizens. This would not only aim at making the administration more responsive but could make it act as a positive change agent for economic and development activities.

Developing Subordinates

No organisation can develop and prosper unless it has a committed and developed workforce. This would be possible only if efforts are made to develop the subordinates in a given system by the head of that unit or sub-system. It holds good for the administrative system's organisations also which are in the existence under a number of nomenclatures throughout the country. If the functionaries are expected to take up the tasks of dealing with citizens with regard to innumerable activities effectively, it is necessary that the heads of such units or sub-systems attempt to create an atmosphere which is considered as conducive by the subordinates. In other words, the top boss must develop his subordinates for giving their best to the organisation.

For getting into the process of developing the subordinates, first of all the leader or the head of the unit must have a proper understanding of his unit's goals, values, climate, culture strengths and weaknesses. This would enable him to clearly know where his unit stands and what he is to do for achieving the goals and objectives by taking his subordinates alongwith him. Furthermore, the understanding of these points would make him develop himself fast. Most of the Indians still accept the leader as their model or ideal and do behave the way they find him behaving. Therefore, it is a must for the leader to firstly develop himself, rather be a model for taking the steps further to develop his subordinates.

It is essential that the employees must own their unit of work and take pride in claiming that they belong to such and such unit of administration. It is possible only if the spirit of belonging is inculcated among the employees. The employees must be convinced that they should be known by their organisation and their organisation should be known by them. How is it possible? The good or bad deeds done by the functionaries only will get a good or bad name for the organisations. Hence, the individuals having the spirit of belonging will attempt their best and work whole-heartedly for their units.

Another step involved in the process of developing subordinates is to ensure decentralised functioning. This point has been discussed at length in the preceding section of this chapter, so we would not be going in details here. But one thing that must always be kept in view is that by and large the functioning should be decentralised providing chance to a number of functionaries to involve them in the process. More and more employees should be made to take crucial decisions so far as their functional aspects are concerned. This would get them closer to each other and make them have more involvement with their organisation. To err is human. It is possible that at times the subordinates may make mistakes in this process and take some wrong decisions. This is a very crucial moment for the employees to come closer to the organisation or get away from it. It will depend upon the attitude of the top boss towards the employees in such situations. The boss should give the employees timely feedback and caution them about any wrong decision rather than punishing them for the same. In case of any good work having been done by them, the boss should never hesitate or delay in recognising and appreciating the action taken by such workers. All this is possible if the boss has an inclination towards making a fair appraisal of the work and not adhering to the negative principles of nepotism, favouritism, and divide and rule.

As discussed earlier, for developing the subordinates it is a must to have sound horizontal and vertical communication networks in operation in the unit. The communication should not only be up-side-down and down-side-up but even among the employees the feelings of group behaviour and social organism have to be inculcated for making them committed to various parts of their organisation. The boss must build and maintain an effective interpersonal relationship with his subordinates. This will amount to better work output from them. The employees must be controlled but for developing the subordinates for the purpose of getting their best it is a must to exercise the minimum control over them and giving them more responsibility. As said earlier, the check could be through constant monitoring that too within the parameters of improving and rewarding their performance and not punishing them for the wrongs. Of course, in cases where some employees keep on repeatedly and intentionally making mistakes, such functionaries should be taken to task severely for sending a message to the others as well that intentional moves to jeopardise or stall the functioning of the organisation are not being tolerated at all. All these simple techniques would make a boss develop his team of workers for the benefit of the administrative organisation, the subordinates, the boss himself, the organisational goals and objectives, and, through all these, the citizens who come in contact with the given unit of the administration. Development of subordinates will make the administration more responsive to the needs, wants, aspirations, and expectations of the citizens.

Adequate Allocation of Resources

With passage of time and the initiatives taken by the government its tasks have increased manifold. As a result more dependence of the citizens on the government is being witnessed. Gone are the days when people used to actively associate with the government for performing some tasks. Now the situation is altogether different. More distance between the administration and the citizens, over the years, is also an important contributing factor for people not actively co-operating with the government for the performance of tasks. Consequently, the activities of the administration have increased not only in size but also in number. It is an admitted fact that for undertaking any activity effectively there would be the requirement of resources. More and more developmental policies and projects have also made governmental agencies feel short of resources. Lack of proper resources with regard to manpower, infrastructural requirements and facilities, etc., result in more delays in the work causing dissatisfaction among the clientele. On the other end, it is strongly felt that the size of bureaucracy has increased beyond the affording capacity of our poor country. Whatever may the reason be, but one thing is sure that lack of resources would not make any agency perform better. There could be two ways of looking at it. One is to let the things happen the way they are unless more resources are provided. It would not only amount to people's dissatisfaction but would also increase the gap between citizens and the administration, besides, affecting the targets to be attained by the government. The other way is to make a proper allocation of available resources in such a way that the maximum output could be there with the minimum of input in the shape of resources. Is it possible in the governmental system? This is a big question, because in a country like India the people by and large, whether citizens or functionaries, do not have any kind of commitment to the nation as such. One can manage even with the least resources when it comes to one's personal interests or aspects but certainly it won't be done when it is the task of the government. The administrative leaders have to take a proper stock and make a careful analysis of the resources available and tasks/objectives to be accomplished/attained. A clear picture of what is to be done and the resources available with them could make them have discussions with their subordinates for finding the ways to deal with the aspects. Within the given resources, even if these are minimum, strategies could be evolved for attaining the objectives, may be in phases to begin with. Adequate allocation of resources, men, material and machinery, could go a long way in achieving something rather than keeping on grumbling and passing the buck from one to another for not being able to do a work because the resources were not sufficient. It could be analysed in different situations as follows:

Situation No. 1 : The area to be covered is more and the resources are not enough to cope with the tasks.

Situation No. 2 : The number of beneficiaries is too much in comparison to the resources available.

Situation No. 3: Area is not much, beneficiaries are also not that many but the items to be taken care of are too many in number.

In Situation 1, where the area is more the solution could be to begin with the task in phases. But it should be made clear to the population in the target area that because of the resource handicap we are covering up the total area in phases. The small teams of individuals alongwith limited facilities should be despatched to the places but it would work effectively only if the people assigned the tasks are spirited and committed to it.

With regard to Situation 2, where beneficiaries are more in number the functionaries can deal with them effectively by having a meaningful way of adopting a token system and getting back to the public in the same order in which the people had approached the agency. First come first served should be the principle and the public must be informed well in advance about the time it would take the functional agency to do the work. Some functionaries should be allotted the duty of scrutinising the papers to be submitted by the people so that at that point only the deficiencies are pointed out and the public is asked to provide required documents. The order of requests should not be disturbed because it sends a wrong message to the public that the administration is biased and works only for those who have influence.

With regard to Situation 3, where neither the area nor the traget group is large but the items included in the package are too many, there is need for effective coordination. The movement of the file should be fast and responsibilities fixed. The limited resources should be so deployed that a good work speed is maintained and the maximum is achieved with the minimum inputs. Daily monitoring of the work would further add on to the output. Under all these situations, by and large, the style of the administrative leader should be participative or democratic alongwith the one whereby his total commitment to the task is revealed. His doing the work himself at times would motivate his subordinates to work much more than they otherwise will do. Depending upon the situation a mechanism should be evolved for allocating the resources for ensuring responsiveness of administration to the needs, wants, demands and genuine expectations of the citizens.

Institution Building

The administrative system and a substantial number of its sub-units are often condemned for not responding to the needs and wants of the citizens and contributing effectively to the overall developmental activities. One seldom appreciates the amount of pressures and compulsions which the functionaries have over them. For instance, the element of transferability is the one which does not permit an administrative functionary to settle down and chalk out his strategies for working and making his subordinates and peers work in accordance with the same. A deep probe into the aspect reveals that the average tenure of an administrative official in state administration is around six months. One of the important reasons for such quantitative frequency in transfers is the day-to-day interference by political leaders. The moment the state government has a change in its political leadership the lists of transfers start appearing everyday. Even this phenomenon has been surpassed now and the moment one administrative official is not able to satisfy the whims of political heavy weights, he gets transferred which not only disturbs his, as well his office's work schedule but demoralises him for not being permitted to do good work or getting demotivated for not fulfilling the nefarious designs of the political bigwigs.

Another factor is out-of-turn promotions and allocating key positions or being deprived of the same irrespective of the principles of seniority and the past service record. All these factors are responsible for making an administrator seriously think of working as per the whims of the political masters and behaving as they wish him to do. The ultimate effect of this is the negativities being reflected in the performance, lack of administrative responsiveness, and an increasing gap between the citizen and the administration.

Man is selfish by nature and necessity. Everyone is basically governed by this principle. But the higher the position of an individual, greater are the expectations of the people and the system of him. The administrators being normal human beings will always have craving for protecting themselves from frequent transfers thus affecting their and their families' lives, and an urge for serving on the key positions, and the desire that their juniors should not be promoted to be their seniors, etc., make them run after the political leaders who have the ultimate power and authority of controlling them. A serious insight into this aspect would probably reveal that administrative functionaries are themselves responsible for this downgradation and lowering down their image and position in the eyes of political leaders. This does not apply only between civil servants, viz., IAS, IPS and State administrative services officials and political leaders, but also between the technocrats and the civil service functionaries.

In the 1950s, for example, the Chief Engineer, PWD, in a State used to be ex-officio Secretary to the State government also. An Executive Engineer used to be given due weightage and regard by the District Collector. The Civil Surgeon used to be considered by the civil service as a top most district level functionary. The Principal of the Government College had a standing of his own and the District Collector used to fix appointment with him before meeting him. The Vice-Chancellor of University used to get much regard from the State Chief Minister. Within the services, now the situation has changed. Everywhere the tussle is between the technocrats and the generalists and the latter, being closer to the game of the 'power quarters', have occupied a place of prominence over the technocrats. The state civil services officials are treated in an inferior manner by the incumbents in the Indian Administrative Services. This aspect does not come to an end here only. The IAS, IPS and State Civil Services officials, the technocrats, the educationists, etc., because of more authority and ultimate power with the political masters, tend to bow down before them. This has resulted in the politicians wielding more and more of unconstitutional power and now the situation is that they consider it to be their right and privilege to interfere in the day-to-day working and the moment they feel that a functionary is not working as per their designs, the particular functionary is made to shift from that position.

The basic cause for the technocrats coming under the dominance of civil services and all the service personnel being cowed down by the political leaders is the lack of institionalisation in the services. By it one means the lack of any professional code of ethics and work to be followed and adhered to by all concerned. Queen Elizabeth was interested in getting some work done by the London Police Commissioner and the wish of Her Majesty was conveyed to the police chief. As it was not within the rules the official did not work as desired. The result was that the functionary was replaced. The successor was also assigned the same task, he did what was done by his predecessor. The second one was also replaced by the third one who again followed the same course which two of his immediate predecessors had done. The total incident was brought to the notice of Her Excellency. She immediately rebuked the agents who had been doing all this and realised her mistake. In India, unfortunately, we have circumstances quite contrary to what is being conveyed through the British example. Here, if one official prefers to stick to the rules and refuses to unlawfully behave in accordance with politicians whims, he gets transferred and his successor though not happy to carry out the task which was refused by his predecessor would feel obliged to act as desired. Our officials keep on running after the powers that be to win favours from them. A senior civil servant in one of the states was once delivering a lecture in a training programme for state college Principals. This officer was once Education Secretary to the state government. As usual some of the participants raised the question of frequent transfers. In reply to it three of the participants in the group were described by the speaker as the ones, of course, without naming them, who had tried to exercise every kind of pressure on the speaker for their transfer. The officials themselves work against their own interest. Why does one always want to be at the place which has good facilities, why the others do not have the same right? If the administrative functionaries strongly build their institution and adopt some code of ethics and norms, the political leadership would not be able to exploit them. Our functionaries run after the political masters to get what is undue and, in turn they would tow the line of the political leaders. If one or two out of one hundred officials attempt to keep his/their identity alive and work as per norms the remaining ninety-nine or ninety-eight look forward to the opportunity of making those one or two to be the scapegoats and in turn occupy the positions held by him/them. Such instances then are often quoted by a sizeable section of officials to terrify the remaining ones. The tragedy is that we don't realise that the victory of evil designs of political force is not because of the lawful power and authority but because of the lack of institutionalism and values in the officials. If all start resisting pressures of the politicians then from whom can they get the illegal work done. Another thing is that the political leaders are not the enemies of the administrative functionaries or vice-versa. Both have to work in such a manner that the best results are achieved in the minimum time. The administrative officials have permanent jobs, little bit of getting away from the temporary allurements relating to self-interest can make them function in the best possible manner adding substantially to the administration's responsiveness.

Dealing with Local Institutions

One of the major objectives of the Indian Constitution is to establish a socialist society and to take care of all irrespective of caste, colour, sex, creed, region, language, etc. As has been a point of reference in the earlier portions of this book, politically elected institutions at the grass-roots were created in order to secure an effective and meaningful participation of the majority of the Indian society in the formulation and execution of such developmental programmes by which there could be a radical improvement in the social and economic conditions of its weaker sections. The Panchayati Raj bodies were brought on the scene to provide a suitable forum for effecting a meaningful participation of these sections -- including the Scheduled Castes and the Scheduled Tribes -- in the local decision-making and the programmes' execution mechanism. These local institutions were to get the required support and assistance from the state administrative set-up for ushering in the developmental activity and maintaining law and order by getting help from these local institutions in the respective jurisdictional areas of these bodies. Commenting upon it, the Draft Five Year Plan, 1978-83, said: "Critical for the success of all redistributive laws, policies and programmes is that the poor be organised and made conscious of the benefits intended for them. Local leaders of the poor have to ensure that all area plans and sectoral plans designed for the benefit of their localities and target groups are effectively administered. The general lesson of the experience so far is that because of leakages in delivery systems and ineffective administration, rural programmes fail to improve the distribution of income. The Planning Commission is proposing a massive shift of resources in favour of rural areas with an in-built redistributive character in almost every programme. But whether the larger resources will have the desired equalising effect will depend on the extent to which the organised pressure of the beneficiaries counteracts the weaknesses of the administration and the opposition of vested interests".

Unfortunately, what the country witnessed with regard to status, relationship and position of local bodies, bureaucracy, and development programmes vis-a-vis each other was rather contrary to the basic concepts of local institutions. The local bodies which are the nursery of political processes in any democratic polity have lost their ground and status. Hardly these are taken seriously by the local administration, local leaders, and local inhabitants. The local administration because of the basic tendency on the part of the administration of usurping powers did not help the local political institutions gain strength. Scores of these bodies have remained either suspended or are often superseded because of both political as well as administrative reasons contradicting the basic utility of the creation of these bodies. Where in existence, a good number of instances are present when the leadership of these bodies had virtually sold the elected forums to the local administration for their petty interests. This has provided an easy handle to the administration to behave as it wants to. The local bodies which were supposed to facilitate the functioning of the administration for being more smooth and responsive could not do anything in this direction. Does this weak stature and position of local elected bodies help the administration?, is a question which needs to be answered logically. The administration may think it to be so. For local inhabitants, it is a sorry state of affairs because it has left them nowhere. Neither have they the elected body to protect their needs nor is the administration open to their expectations and wants. Hence, the gap between the citizen and administration is increasing everyday.

The administration, if it is keen to work for the betterment of the citizens, should try to strengthen the hands of the local bodies. These bodies could put forward those policies and programmes which suit the needs of their areas and inhabitants in a better manner. On the one hand, by doing so the administration would do what is needed by the area and its inhabitants and, on the other, it would convey a message to the citizens that the administration cares for it, hence reducing the number of grievances and complaints.

The administration should never attempt to please a few top local leaders for serving such interests which are not for the good of the masses. The administration should rather encourage the democratic processes to take place in a proper and qualitative order. Never should the local institutions functioning be jeopardised by the administration. Proper functioning of these bodies would also be a check on the performance of the administration and could thus make it function in a better manner.

Dealing with Political Leaders

Independent India has its commitment to the establishment of a welfare state. The Directive Principles enshrined in the Constitution seek to ensure the emergence of a socialistic society while avoiding concentration of wealth and means of production in the hands of few. The governmental process comprises two important aspects : one is policy-making and the other is its execution. The political masters have the duty to work out policies whereby the maximum benefits go to the maximum number of people. Of course, the political masters get the support of the permanent executive in framing these policies. The basic role of the administration is to implement the policies thus framed by the political executive. These policies are meant to be executed for the benefit of the public in whose name the entire machine of the government is put to gears.

The present scenario is one wherein political leaders blame the administration and the administration blames the politicians and citizens and on the other end the citizens blame both the political masters as well as administrative functionaries for an improper implementation of policies, corruption, nepotism, red-tapism, etc. There is complete lack of faith in each other.

The administrators feel that political leaders' abundant interference does not permit them to work properly. The politicians feel that they have been elected by the people and thus are more responsible to protect their interests and for safeguarding the same they have to exercise check upon the administration.

What is required is a well chalked out mechanism where both the political leaders and the administration could work for the betterment of the masses. Both should not attempt to just point out the deficiencies of each other. In fact, there can not be any conflict between the two if each thinks of the other as its supporting partner rather than an opponent as it is in the prevailing situation.

The administrators can get support from the political leaders for performing their duties in a better way if they attempt to appreciate the position of the political leaders. There is no denying the fact that the political leaders have occupied the place of governance because of the support of the public and so are to protect their interests. It is in the interest of the politicians themselves as well as that of their parties because they have to go to the public again after a stipulated period for seeking their mandate. The administrators should attempt to work on the lines being suggested by the political leaders. Does it mean that they should carry out what the political leaders tell them to do? Certainty not! If asked to do what is wrong, the administrators should explain the problems and the rules and regulations to the politicians in a polite but firm way. But obviously this should not be the case with regard to even the just cases. The political leaders are in the know of the importance of the administrative functionaries in so far as the implementation is concerned. The orders of only the administration could get the things move. Whatever is not judicious should be explained to the political leaders and they should be told that going the other way round could rather spoil the reputation of the politicians as well as of their parties. Most of the so called interference of political leaders in administrative work is with regard to prompt action to be taken in routine cases. In such events the chances of the politicians to interfere could be substantially decreased if there is quick disposal of cases and the administration works in a fair manner alongwith making impartial decisions. All this could happen only if the administrative functionaries are wedded to the idea of effective and efficient functioning without showing any desire of doing away with the rules in some selected cases of the few being closer to or liked by the said functionaries. Undue pressure in illegal matters from the politicians should completely be resisted by the administrators. Once an administrator has the reputation of doing what is just and resisting the pressures of any magnitude would leave little scope of his being bothered again and again by the political leaders. Such functioning would go a long way in making the administration responsive to the common man without the people developing a grudge against the administrative functionaries in particular and the administrative system in general.

Dealing with Citizens

Everything in a democratic polity exists for the benefit and welfare of the citizens. Complete government infrastructure, apparatus, and machinery is meant to be utilized to get to the citizens not only whatever is their due but much more than that. The administrative system has the overall responsibility of translating into action all the programmes framed by the government for the benefit and welfare of the citizens. Over the years the government has taken almost complete charge of things regarding human life under its fold which has increased the dependence of the people on the administration. On the one hand, the people look towards the administration for each and everything and, on the other, the common people feel that they are not being looked after by the administration properly. The distance between the administration and the people is increasing everyday as a result of which citizens hardly have any faith and trust in today's administration.

The administrative system has to be improved upon and basically it becomes the primary obligation of the constituents of this system to do so by putting in their best and seeking cooperation of others for doing so. The following few points can help reduce the gap between the two and also make administration more responsive.

Firstly, the administration through all possible and available means, should publicize and propagate the policies and programmes of the government among the people. It should clearly identify the specific target group or groups and area or areas being covered by a particular programme or policy. Not only this, efforts must be made to let people know the way of getting the benefits of the same, the procedure for it and the possible time which the agency would take when approached by the beneficiary for the work to be done. This would not only reduce the number of people going to the offices knowing that the benefits of a particular policy are not meant for them but would enable them to know beforehand the right way and procedure for seeking the benefit if available to them. As a result of it, not only would the administration's credibility be built up but the public time would also be saved.

Secondly, the administrative agencies must give a serious thought to the aspect of the citizens getting proper attention whenever they approach the agency. One of the major criticisms of the administration is that the administration does not bother about the citizens and none in the agency/office has any time to talk to the people and guide them properly. A large number of persons try to find out one source or the other for the purpose of getting some information from the offices. Discourtesy on the part of office functionaries adds fuel to the fire. The government agencies having the responsibility of dealing with the public must deploy some of its trained and well informed persons at the reception counters and all the citizens should be given every information and guidance regarding procedures for getting the benefits. This would help not only the citizens but also the functionaries as untargeted groups' requestes, applications, and queries would not be reaching them thus increasing their efficiency to work for the actual beneficiaries of the policy.

Thirdly, service agencies of the administration should make efficient working the cornerstone of their functioning. Benefits should reach the public not only speedily but also effectively. Half the charm of a specific benefit goes if it reaches the concerned quarters after delays and frantic efforts. Besides winning the confidence and help from the citizens, it would amount to decrease in a large quantity, the pressures being exercised by the citizens on the administration through politicians and administrative superiors. Furthermore, such agencies should ensure that people are not put to troubles or hazards.

Fourthly, the administration must adhere strictly to the principle of equality. In other words, all the beneficiaries or clients should be treated as equals without giving favours to one or few among the target group. Such an attitude conveys the message that the administration is biased and works for those who have at their back some influencing factor, may it be a politician, a senior bureaucrat, a relation of the functionary, or even money.

Fifthly, the heads of the administrative units should clearly state the time specifically earmarked in their everyday schedule for meeting people and listening to their problems and difficulties. It would not only help the people in getting their due but would be of great help to the administrative head for having a proper feedback about the functioning of his unit for the purpose of bringing improvements in the same. The daily time for meeting the public should be utilized properly and a business-minded approach adopted. More and more people should be heard and quick action taken on their requests. The action should not only be taken but also conveyed to the concerned as early as possible.

Sixthly, the heads of the administrative agencies should make more frequent tours of their respective jurisdictional areas. It would help them not only meet more and more of citizens but also to know about the actual performance of their units. With passage of time, night touring halts outside the headquarters being made by the administrators are decreasing. The administrator must come out to see what is happening and what problems the people are facing. It would lead to reducing the complaints/grievances received by the office at headquarters -- be it a district, a sub-division, or a block -- as the officer concerned would be taking action on the spot. Besides this, it would make an administrator anticipate a problem in times to come and he could take timely action to either let the same not happen or adopt measures well in advance to meet the problem speedily and effectively.

Seventhly, the administration must make it a point to explain its hardships, constraints, and problems to the public. There is no fun telling a person to come after two days when you know his work can not be done in even fifteen days time. The administration need not feel shy in accepting and rather telling people that because of such and such problem the delay would be there. Keeping a person in dark and making him come to the office every second day for seven times would not only put the person to unnecessary botheration but he would be bothering the functionaries as well by coming to them time and again.

The administration is expected to work for the people with more efficiency, effectiveness, and courtesy. The administrative units heads should attempt to educate the public through small group meetings, political leaders, voluntary organisations, non-governmental organisations and meeting citizens in their offices, and outside, about the problems and mechanism of its working for eliciting maximum support from the citizens. Citizens' co-operation is a must for making the administration responsive. At present the common citizen is not educated and aware enough to offer his co-operation whereas the administrators are capable of seeking the same from the public by way of their functioning, behaviour, and apparently show concern for the citizens ultimately for the benefit and welfare of whom the administration is existing.

In the preceding sixteen sub-sections of this chapter the focus of discussion and analysis has been on some of the important techniques which could help improve the administrative system for the purpose of the same being oriented to the needs of the citizens. Though there are some other ways also to be adopted for the purpose, yet basically the techniques which could prove to be more useful in most of the given situations have been analysed. By and large, all these techniques are revolving around the functionaries and the top bosses in various subunits and sub-systems of administrative organisations because it is primarily the individuals-at-work in a system who mean a lot for making the system good or bad or, in other words, for coming out with fruitful results even while having a scarcity of resources in some situations. In the subsequent chapter the focus of discussion would be on the perceptions of some of the top political leaders and administrators regarding making the administration more responsive to the needs, wants, and aspirations of the society at large.

References

1. Selznick, Philip, *Leadership in Administration,* New York, Harper and Row, 1956, p-29.
2. Terry, George R., *Principles of Management,* Homewood, Richard D. Irwin, 1960, pp. 11-12.
3. Tannenbaum , Robert et al., *Leadership and Organisation : A Behavioural Science Approach,* New York, McGraw-Hill, 1961, p. 8.

4. Koontz, Harold and C. O'Donnell, *Principles of Management*, New York, McGraw Hill, 1961, p. 23.
5. Stogdill, Ralph M., "Personal Factors Associated with Leadership: A Survey of the Literature", *The Journal of Psychology*, USA, 1948.
6. Ghiselli, Edwin E., "Management Talent", *American Psychologist*, USA, 1963.
7. Tannenbaum, Robert et al., *op.cit.*, pp. 107-10.
8. *Ibid.*
9. Blake, Robert R. and Jane S. Mouton, "Managerial Facades", *Advanced Management Journal*, USA, 1966.
10. Reddin, William J., "Managing Organisational Change", *Personnel Journal*, USA, 1969.
11. *Ibid.*
12. *Ibid.*
13. Simon, Herbert A., *The New Science of Management Decision*, New York, Harper, 1960, p. 2.
14. Kolasa, Blair J., *Introduction to Behavioural Science for Business*, New Delhi, Wiley Eastern, 1970, p. 228.
15. Katz, D. et al., *Productivity Supervision, and Morale in an Office Situation*, Ann Arbor, Michigan University Press, 1950, pp. 39-41.
16. Turner, A.N. and P.R. Lawrence, *Industrial Jobs and the Worker*, Boston, Harvard University Press, 1965, pp. 57-61.
17. Vroom, V.H., "The Effects of Attitudes on Perception of Organisational Goals", *Human Relations*, USA, 1960.
18. Simon, H.A., "On the Concept of Organizational Goal", *Administrative Science Quarterly*, USA, 1964.
19. Steer, R.M., *Organizational Effectiveness : A Behavioural View*, California, Santa Monica, 1977, pp. 88-94.
20. Locke, E.A., "Toward a Theory of Task Motivation and Incentives", *Organizational Behaviour and Human Performance*, USA, 1968.
21. Albers, Henry H., *Principles of Management*, Wiley, New York, 1969, p. 186.
22. Duncan, Robert, "What is the Right Organization Structure?", in *Organizational Dynamics*, USA, 1976.
23. *Ibid.*
24. Vardaman, George T. and Carroll C. Hulterman, *Managerial Control Through Communications*, New York, Wiley, 1968. pp. 3-4.
25. Haimann, Theo, *Professional Manager*, Boston, Houghton Miffins, 1962, p. 27.
26. Weber, Max, *The Theory of Social and Economic Organisations*, London, The Free Press, 1948.
27. Tead, Ordway, *The Art of Administration*, New York, Harper and Row, 1951, p. 192.

28. Maslow, Abraham, *Motivation and Personality*, New York, Harper and Row, 1954, pp. 21-37.
29. Herzberg, Frederick et al., *The Motivation to Work*, New York, John Wiley and Sons, 1959, pp. 53-59.
30. McDougall, William, *An Introduction to Social Psychology*, Boston, Luce, 1914, pp. 83-87.
31. McClelland, Davis, *The Achieving Society*, New York, Von-Zostrand, 1961, pp. 11-15.

3

Some Perceptions

A person who approaches the office for a job is called a job seeker or a job hunter. When he gets it, he has to come up to the expectations of the job, of the clientele which he is supposed to serve, of that organisation which he was striving to join, and of the administrative system and polity at large. He has to become a conscientious individual who is responsible to the system, to the state, to the nation and is to develop an attitude whereby he becomes responsible and answerable to his own self as well because a responsible administration would come out only of responsible people. Somehow or the other, the functionaries in Indian administration do not respond to the needs of the nation.

It would not be wrong to say that our administration is not humanized. Take the example of a file which is about some issue pertaining to somebody. What would make the file alive is the man at the file. If he is alive, the file is alive and if he is dead, the file is more so. Unfortunately, what appears on the Indian scene is that the man at the file is more lifeless than the file itself. It seems, in majority of the cases, that the man in administration has not much concern and he takes his own time for dealing with each and every case. Such a callous attitude on the part of administrative functionaries is classic and true of India alone as nowhere in the world there is such an attitude. In most other countries, the administrative officials try to do immediately what is expected by a fair person. Such responsiveness is rare to come by in India. Probably there is no human response. Instead of solving the problem which a citizen has brought to an official, he will look to the letter of the law, he will find ways to point out that the application is not properly worded and hence would throw the application on the face of the applicant. By all means, what is required is not such an attitude but a positive one implying that the official is there to advise the applicant to write a proper application, etc. Such a system is called humanistic administration or administration with a human face. Right from the Central Secretariat down to the village panchayat the administration must possess intense humanity as it is dealing with people face to face.

R. Venkataraman has depicted the picture of the bureaucrat he used to study in his early days, as[1]:

> "One seldom sees a Bureaucrat
> Without a pipe or with a hat
> His habitat is corridors
> He takes his exercise indoors
> He is always somewhere in between
> Two meetings where he should have been
> His favourite words are Activate
> Co-ordinate, Evaluate.
> He can't afford to be precise
> Indignant, Adamant, Concise
> A Bureaucrat is seldom seen
> Without a pen or with a dream".

The present-day bureaucrat cannot afford to be like the one described above. He requires a new repertoire of knowledge and skills, supported by a new set of attitudes and values which can comprehend realities and react to the changing environment. But do we find an administration which has adopted such a kind of change in the attitude and performance of the individuals at work at different places and at different levels in the administrative system? In majority of the cases, the answer would straightaway be 'NO!' with capital letters.

The state of administration in the country is actually very miserable. A good number of studies have been conducted revealing the performance of the administrative institutions as far from satisfactory levels. One of the important reasons for the same is the attitude of the functionaries or the basic commitment of the organisationalists to their organisations, its goals, and its clientele.

As per the data of the government, on an average, various central government departments and ministries receive about 13 lakh complaints from the public every year. The complaints are mostly regarding the misbehaviour of officials, harassment being faced by the people, delay in action, lack of information supplied, poor and improper service rendered by the governmental agencies and delay in settling issues of family pension, gratuity, etc. The maximum number of complaints are received by the finance (banking), communications, railways and defence. The grievances are disposed of, but the administrative unit does not specify what it means by disposal, nor does it keep track of repeat complaints. The Estimate Committee of the Parliament made an indepth study of the Directorate of Public Grievances set up as an independent agency under the Cabinet Secretariat. It found that out of 300-350 complaints recieved by it every month, only 26 per cent of the accepted cases were decided. The Directorate also rejects the cases as "frivolus". Half of the cases decided take more than three months to be sorted out. The committee said, "this is not a happy score for an institution which has been set up to create a sense of confidence among the public with regard to the functioning of the government".[2] The Committee has recommended that the Directorate be converted into a statutory authority on the pattern of an Ombudsman in Scandinavian countries.

Commenting upon the administration as a machine for the transformation and the bureaucracy as the engine of continuity and change, Rajiv Gandhi, the former Prime Minister of India said, "Too often I find that the bureaucracy is closed upto its own little boxes. If you are looking at energy, then you are not sensitive to any other development that is taking place and your attention is totally concentrated in that one sphere. If you are in some other sphere, then it is totally on that. There is a very great need for the bureaucracy to look across these walls into what is happening in other departments, into the totality of development, into the direction that the country is going. . . . The District Magistrate or Collector is the Government as far as the people are concerned, with a capital `G'. The face that you present to the millions you come in contact with is the face of the government. Your behaviour is the behaviour of the government, your attitude is the attitude of the government. Your concern for the poor and the deprived is the concern of the government. And, again, it is your achievement of the targets that are set which is the achievement of the government". . .[3]

Addressing the District Collectors, he said, "You should be taking a hard look at the interface between the administration and the people, the administration and the political level, in the light of your personal experience and that of all of your colleagues from all parts of the country. Through this process you and me, both, will gain an invaluable insight into how the administration can be made more responsive. You will examine how policy directives which come from the political level get translated into actual action, and see how the people's perceptions of their problems can be reflected in the programmes''.[4] He further said: ''We cannot achieve this by mere exhortation or policy pronouncements. It can only be done if we address ourselves to the specific problems, to the specific questions to get specific answers. You have to ask yourself whether or not to propose a course of action which strengthens the forces of unity and harmony while simultaneously promoting the celebration of our diversity''.[5]

While admitting the fact that no government can function without rules, the Indian Prime Minister, Mr. P.V. Narasimha Rao, said that the ''rules should be such as to provide succour to the common man and not hinder development''. He stated that ''the capacity to interpret the rules to block development was more in evidence in the country. Each time an attempt was made to simplify the procedures, they got more complicated because the administrators did not want the system to change''. He holds the view that the rules should be redrafted in a simple language so that the common man could understand the working of the government. The Prime Minister is of the opinion that the bureaucrats who are not prepared to change their outlook and administrative procedures are blocking the implementation of the policies of the government[6].

The statements of facts, realities and observations made in the above sections reveal the state of India's administration and the role played by the administrative functionaries adding to the lack of responsiveness of the administration. For the purpose of this study, we interviewed some of the political leaders and administrators to elicit their views and perceptions of administrative responsiveness and various facets related to it in the context of Indian polity and administration. The perceptions and views of the political leaders followed by those of the administrators are mentioned in the succeeding text in an alphabetical order. The perceptions have been categorised as under:-

I. Politicians' perceptions of Indian administration and administrative responsiveness

II. Administrators' perceptions of Indian administration and administrative responsiveness.

III. (a) Politicians' perceptions of political leaders interference.
(b) Politicians' perceptions of training of political leaders.

IV. Administrators' perceptions of political leaders interference in administration.

V. Politicians' perceptions of improving administrative responsiveness.

VI. Administrators' perceptions of improving administrative responsiveness.

I. Politicians Perceptions of Indian Administration and Administrative Responsiveness

Harkishan Singh Surjeet, General Secretary, Communist Party of India (Marxist) while expressing his perception of administrative responsiveness in India says:

''First important question is that after independence people expected a big change in the administrative response: reason being the British had their own purpose, because to rule the country they wanted to pursue so many things which were alienating the people more and more. The independent country required response on the part of administration in such a way that people feel (*sic*) administration a part and parcel of their life meant to resolve the problems which they are facing whether in sphere of administration, law and order or in the developmental activities. But now during this present 45 years slowly there has been degeneration and people's experience is quite different.

''Two factors are there which have been responsible for such situation which has been created. In the early days, we carried forward the administration which we inherited from the Britishers but, subsequently, it has been multiplied in such a way where inefficiency has come in instead of efficiency. Compare each government department now with the British times, you will find the number of people engaged in each has increased considerably.

''For a developing country like that of India, half of the budget is spent on the administrative staff itself and this is by all means a big burden on our exchequer. On the top of it, the administration has become inept and ineffectual. If you go to an office you will find every body complaining there. My file is not moving, it goes from one desk to another.

''I have my own experience. Recently we have built a new office in New Delhi. We are a recognized political party with more than 50 members in the Parliament. Since one month, I am not getting electricity connection. I finally requested Amal Dutta, M.P. to meet the concerned Executive Engineer. He was told by the officer to go to some other functionaries of his department. After moving from this end to the other now they havē promised that within one month they would be able to do this. You can well imagine that if this is the fate of the party like ours which has got tremendous influence then what happens to a common man. Layers and layers have developed in the administration which is not only a burden on the exchequer but has also amounted to its inefficiency.

" Another aspect, which I have noticed, is that our administration is not people-oriented, development-oriented, oriented towards fulfilling the goals which are enshrined in our Constitution. But instead of doing so our administrators have copied the pattern from British, which has led to further alienation from the people, they don't feel that the relationship with people should be such whereby people feel that this is our own administration, we can get our grievances redressed, we can get our problems solved, we can enter into development activities and all that.

"The administration has developed vested interest and that comes in the way of reducing the gap between the people and the administration. For example, in Punjab, I can tell you the people now are fed up with the extremists and the separatists. At the same time, the administration is so much alienated from the people that they don't expect any good action from police and the administration. Instead of making use of people's discontentment against the extremists and separatists and to rally them in the struggle to the unity of the state and the country, the administration is intentionally not moving in right directions and is rather illtreating the masses because of its vested interest in the continuation of President's rule. It is they who are ruling. No other political force counts, they are making money and adopting all possible corrupt means to suit their convenience.

"One positive element was there in the British Administration. The positive element was that though they were biased against national movement, yet in other activities they tried to judge on the basis of some principles. This worked for some time after independence but subsequently what has happened is that various political forces started appearing on the scene of power in the states and the officers also entered into a kind of compromise with political leaders at the cost of principles and credibility of the system and administration. They are not loyal to the Constitution, to the job, but to the individual politicians and political parties. Every officer is one who is a person of so and so and I have seen major political parties which are more interested in the appointments of their chums at influential positions. Similarly, it is true of leaders at the lower levels. If a Sub-Inspector of their choice is posted at their place they are satisfied, all their grievances are over".

Commenting upon the hope for betterment, Surjeet stated: "If the country has to resolve (*sic*) to meaningful development, good administration, and effective democratic structure then the radical orientation is required so far as administration is concerned. First and foremost, such a heavy administration is not at all required. Secondly, they should be tuned to, and their promotions should be judged by the performance in relation to the job which is assigned to them. Thirdly, their loyalty should be to the government, and Constitution and not to any individual or group of individuals. Fourthly, the political leaders, especially those in power, should attempt to refrain from making use of cheap tactics.

"Whenever there is change in the political executive, there is quantitative change in the administration. This is something like demoralising the few honest and upright officers and functionaries who get transferred because their colleagues serve those interests of the political bosses which they don't as per rules, so they replace these straight working officials. What is the fault of the administration? Why bulk transfers are ordered every now and then? I quote the example of Punjab again. In 1967, Gurnam Singh became the Chief Minister of Punjab. I was then the Chairman of the Committee of all parties which were running the Government. I suggested to Gurnam Singh to select two persons of his choice, the Chief Secretary and the Principal Secretary to the Chief Minister and not to make wholesale changes because the administration is to serve whichever political party comes to power so they should not be politicised. I told him that doing contrary to my suggestion, he would be just dividing the administration and making a section of it hostile to his government's functioning. Gurnam Singh adhered to my suggestion and for about a year when his government was in power he got the confidence of all. It is, therefore, required that some principles have to be adhered to for bringing the required change and for making administration responsive".

Coming down heavily on the administration and its lack of responsiveness to even genuine needs, wants, and just expectations of the common man in the Indian society, Indrajit Gupta, General

Secretary, Communist Party of India, briefly but forcefully stated during a personal interview:

"Administrative responsiveness is very unsatisfactory. Common citizens do not regard the administration as a custodian of their rights, but, rather as a callous and bureaucratic structure which thrives on corruption. Conscientious officials are the exception not the rule. Administrative functionaries are yet to get out of the bureaucratic mould imparted by long years of the pre-independence colonial rule. Commitment to serving the people is very weak. The most naked example is the police administration which is fast becoming a synonym for corruption, coercion, and terror. The biggest casualty is the law, its enforcement and impartiality".

A senior parliamentarian and formerly Minister in the Union Government, K.C. Pant, belonging to the Congress-I Party, talked about the lack of people's involvement in the administrative working; growing distance between the citizens and administration, and the plight of citizens vis-a-vis the administration. He stated:

"We have gone through different phases since independence. Initially, it was only to have status-quo administration but with the passage of time the government's keen concern was aimed at more and more development in all the fields. We had to be self-sufficient not only in agricultural but in industrial sectors as well. So to cope with it a new kind of administrative structure emerged for providing impetus to development. In the beginning, there was involvement and I remember in the period immediately following independence, there was contribution of labour by people to build roads, to build schools and so on in rural areas. It was *shramdan* but gradually the attitude of the government bearing the full responsibility of the development grew. With it the bureaucracy started getting away from the commoners.

"It has to be analysed why this happened, why the bureaucracy did not have responsiveness: May be it was because of some flaw in the training courses of the bureaucracy but the distance between the administration and people became more and more? I do not know how this attitude developed but over a period of time the involvement of the people in development was not as much as in the beginning and the feeling that public funds and public works have a certain sanctity and rightly related to the welfare of the people was not felt strongly and clearly".

Commenting upon the attitude of the administration towards citizens, Pant observed: "At the cutting edge of the administration, the common man encounters generally indifference and delay and he tends to judge entire administrative machinery from his own experience. A man who has a problem first goes to the administrative institution that is available to him and then if he is strong enough and if he has the resources and he does not get what he considers to be the justice then he goes to the court of law. That in most cases take so long that he is not satisfied with the result and very often he does not in any case get justice. If he goes to the police, there also in many cases, the response is not as expected. Now, it may be that in some cases the bureaucrats or the government officers don't perform judiciously. But there are officers who do their best also. I have come across cases of both good and bad. I do not want to run down the entire administrative machinery, it would be unfair to do so. But the general response is not what people expect and there is an element of wielding power of granting favours to common citizens rather than seeing that the administration serves people. On the other hand, there are people who want to take advantage of the administrative machinery and get something that they will not get under the normal rule. In short, it is a situation in which one has to consciously work towards functioning according to the rule of law and not on the basis of equality before law. And if these two principles could be translated into daily action and the administration performs speedily it would help it to be responsive to the problems of those who are the weakest and who, therefore, have no other recourse except to go to the administration for protection of their rights. That is there where the system could be certainly working well".

Bhartiya Janata Party stalwart and presently leader of the opposition in the Lok Sabha, L.K. Advani, when asked to give his views on responsiveness of the administration pointed out some basic defects which are responsible for the administration not being able to perform in a responsive manner. He said:

"There was a time when responsiveness on the part of administration was perhaps the strongest point of the administration and, therefore, it was known as the steelframe. So much so that when India became independent the first government of free India had no other alternative than to depend upon the bureaucracy which was supposed to be loyal to the foreign masters. Despite that at least the person who was principally decisive in this matter, Sardar Patel, had faith in the fact that the bureaucracy in Indian government brought up in the British tradition would be inclined to be apolitical, politically neutral, and so whatever talents or qualities they had, which they were using earlier for the British masters, with the change in the Government their talents would be made available by them to the new masters as well. The administration did work accordingly and that is the reason that if we tend to compare present -day administration with that of those days one finds the performance on the part of that day administration much satisfactory. My broad perception is that until the early 1970s, this situation was there, and the administration was by and large apolitical and it essentially regarded its responsibility to carry out the policies of whichever Government came to office. Of course, for the first 20 years or 25 years of independence, there were no political changes of a very high magnitude. It was a one party dominance setup. So that was put to the test.

"But my feeling is that in the early 70s there was a conscious attempt on the part of the Government to inject a kind of political commitment into the bureaucracy. They did not confine it only to the bureaucracy. It was brought to judiciary also, the famous supersession of Supreme Court judges led to the advancement of a formal rationale in Parliament that we must have a judiciary which is committed to the political philosophy of the government in office. Though nothing specific in this regard was said about bureaucracy, yet, by and large, the approach with relation to it also was the same. And I think that is the point from which there has been a consistent decline and the administration has started behaving the way it likes without caring for the interests of the citizens at large".

Ram Jethmalani, Member Parliament, and leading jurist has held poor training and lack of motivation on the part of administrative functionaries responsible for lack of responsiveness of the administration. In his words, "Administrative responsiveness, in my judgement, is extremely poor, poor because the administrators do not have sufficient degree of motivation. They are not even properly trained and the kind of training and inspiration that they have got from their superiors is of terribly wrong kind. I don't think that the bigwigs in our politics and administration have distinguished themselves for any integrity or character. So this kind of thing percolates down to the lowest level of administration and all the functionaries from top to bottom are busy in making money, few honourable exceptions apart, but, by and large, it is a very dismal and corrupt scene. I would not say that our administration is in good shape at all".

An economist by profession joining politics later on and becoming a Minister in the Union Cabinet, Subramaniam Swamy, President of the Janata Party, while admitting that the responsiveness of administration is missing has attributed it to the lack of will and clarity on the part of the political executive. He believes that by doing so the political executive can improve upon the administration. He stated:

"This particular system can deliver goods if the Minister has clarity about the job and makes independent decisions. Most of the problems are felt when the Minister does not want to take the responsibility for a decision which even he wanted to take. I mean, he wants a decision in a particular manner but does not want to take the responsibility on him. He usually forces the civil service to put up the file in a specified way so that he could concur with a decision of his liking and choice. When I was Commerce Minister or Law Minister, I used to say that the file should come to me as it is or may be in the way the civil service wanted to send the same. Either I used to overrule the bureaucracy or would go as per their suggestions but the ultimate responsibility was that of mine. As a result of it, I found there was a great deal of efficiency and responsiveness on the part of functionaries attached with my portfolio".

Answering the subsequent question stemming out of the response of Subramaniam Swamy to the effect that the political leadership can mould the things, he remarked emphatically:

"Yes, if the Minister is clear and willing to take final responsibility, even this system can work. Of course, there is also great deal of streamlining required. The workload is too much, employment problem is there, promotional avenues are limited, so these problems are there which if sorted out little intelligently can help produce quality results. But I will say even the present administrative system can respond if the minister is clear and he takes responsibility on the file for the final decision".

Formerly Union Finance Minister, Yashwant Sinha of Samajwadi Janata Party, who had been in the Indian Administrative Service and is now a member of the Rajya Sabha felt that the responsiveness on the part of an administrative functionary was primarily dependent upon his training and attitudinal variable. In his words:

"My first reaction is that responsiveness is largely dependent on how a person has been brought up, what is his attitude in life and what kind of training he has received. Because you will find that in same situation one person is very responsive and the other is not responsive. I am referring to the various constituted cadres. For instance, in the administration, if one makes a micro analysis one finds that people have behaved very differently from one end of the spectrum to another end of the spectrum: in the sense that some people have been very responsive and some people have been very aloof and callous and not responsive at all. There is no denying the fact that responsiveness on the part of the administration is absolutely essential because no administration can be effective without being responsive and unfortunately, we lack it in India. The point is that we have to be very conscious of the personality factor and while a general training will do there is a need for training each individual and making sure that he becomes responsive as long as he is in the administration".

In reply to a question as to whether it could be possible through training or there should be some code of ethics from the government, Sinha said, "There should be a code of ethics from the government side, that again is general. Every officer, whatever his department or station in life is should be told that he must respond. As I said that people have been callous, so such a code will definitely help to supervise and inspect what the officer is doing. What I was referring to was some kind of personal dossier where the responsiveness aspect is clearly commented upon by the senior supervising officers. And if the subordinate is found wanting then he should be trained or put through a special programme so that he becomes more responsive. The advantages of responsiveness are explained to him and he is told what exactly is going on. So, while recognising the merit of a general approach, I am at the same time advocating for an individual approach whereby each functionary should be treated as an entity and he should be tackled as such to enable him to perform in the best interest of the system, society and its constituents".

II. Administrators Perceptions of Indian Administration and Administrative Responsiveness

B.B. Vohra, a senior IAS officer having a distinguished civil service career, opined that the vested interests of the political masters, administrators, and citizens have become so powerful now that in a substantial manner these stand in the way of the administrators to respond to their administrative duties properly. While comparing the present-day administration with that of the pre-independent India, he said:

"Indian administration had a very fine record and traditions of responsiveness towards citizens. During British days except when the demand for independence came in on practically all other matters there was a great deal of responsiveness. District officers felt it to be their duty to tour intensively in the villages, listened to grievances of the people and tried to redress those grievances on the spot. In Punjab this was a very great tradition created by the Lawrence brothers. We were supposed to go to the spot as quickly as possible and sort things out and see that no injustice was done. But I am afraid these traditions have now very largely disappeared and vested interests have become so strong and so well entrenched that the administrator who dares to go against them does so at this own risk".

G. Ram Reddy has vast teaching, research and administrative experience of managing different Universities as Vice-Chancellor to his credit. He is presently Chairman of the University Grants Commission. On the basis of the various research studies he conducted at the grassroots level and his administrative experience, he feels that Indian bureaucracy is indifferent to the expectations of the people, it is more rule-oriented, and cautious than required. He has observed:

"The general complaint in the Indian administration is that bureaucracy is not responsive. This is the complaint at all levels. In fact, people go to the extent of saying that the administration is indifferent to the needs of the people, so that is the general perception and this needs to be improved. Bureaucracy as you know, is governed by rules and regulations and they tend to be very cautious. Bureaucrats don't want to commit any mistakes. As a result they go on raising queries and this leads to lot of delay. People are certainly not happy with this.

"If bureaucracy is responsive, things would improve but that means they must take the initiative, it means that they should be prepared to own a few mistakes and society or their bosses should be able to understand the mistakes and tolerate them, otherwise bureaucracy would continue to be indifferent to the needs of the people".

G. Ram Reddy holds the view very strongly that there has been too much of reliance on bureaucracy. He says, "If bureaucracy is responsive lots of social changes can be brought about. Unfortunately, we, in this country, have relied too much on bureaucracy to bring about changes, which is not the right thing to do. First of all, bureaucracy is not the right agent to bring about changes. We should have minimum reliance on the bureaucracy, otherwise their jobs are permanent, and they tend to be conservative element in the society".

H.D. Shourie, a retired IAS officer, presently running a voluntary organisation called 'Common Cause' is of the view that the administration is not responsive to the citizens. He considers rules, regulations office procedures and an enormous proliferation of the areas in which the government is functioning responsible for the same. He says, "I would like to recount some of the problems which come to my mind straightaway, which are experienced by the strata of society in the urban areas and also in the rural areas. Let us take a few examples so that these could illustrate the problems of the administrative responsiveness also to the people or from the people to the administration. Let me give you one example and that is relating to the requirement which is very often incorporated in prescribed forms for securing attestation by a Gazetted Officer.

"Now imagine the circumstances of an old pensioner or the agriculturist coming from the rural area or a widow who wants to submit a form. Do you think that they will be ever able to get a declaration attested? You go to the Magistrate and the Magistrate says, 'Why have you come, I have no time'. You go to a Gazetted Officer. Where is a Gazetted Officer? With the result, a person is put to such enormous inconvenience that one can't imagine? Now these are types of things arising from this absurdness. I wrote to people all over the country to send me such cases which show exasperations experienced by the people. I received enormous number of letters from various types of resources from all over the country. A man says, 'I am a handicapped person. I applied for travel by rail from such and such place to such and such place and there is a concession available for the handicapped persons. I applied for that concession for the rail ticket. The Babu says, no!, you have to get a certificate attested by a Gazetted Officer that you are handicapped'. He said I am handicapped, look at this I have my leg amputated: he said, no, you get a certificate attested by a Gazetted Officer and then only come back to me'. Another person wrote to me that he had applied to the marriage registrar for getting a certificate of marriage of his daughter and son-in-law, who had got married a week earlier in an Arya Samaj Mandir of the same town. He said, 'I went to this registrar and the Registrar says, no, we cannot do anything. We do not recognise Arya Samaj Mandir'. He said, 'I have got witnesses, those witnesses were present there. He said no! Marriage Registrar was not present there.' How can you converse in a country where you have to get a Marriage Registrar to perform every marriage and only then it will be certified? The person further said that he came out and in the varandah the chaprasi of the officer met him. And he said, 'don't worry, give Rs. 800, everything will be done; out of Rs. 800, Rs. 500 will go to the Registrar and Rs.300 will come to me and you will get the certificate in 15 minutes'. Well, this is type of operation that is going on.

"Let me give you one more example of the administrative problems which are encountered by the people as created by the staff. A person said he could not get the copies of the death certificate in relation to his mother's death. He needed those for purposes of some insurance, etc., which he cannot get unless he submits seven copies of the certificate. Those people wanted the original certificate. The original certificate means that all of them should be original and not photo-copies. He said he had gone to the municipal office and the municipal office people said that it was the rule that they could not issue more than two copies. Now, tell me, he is prepared to pay to get the copies about the demise of his mother but he cannot get the certificate. What, I am advocating is that somehow or the other we have to look at the problems at a micro level".

Shourie says that he would not hold it as either a legacy of the British times or a lukeworm response of the administration responsible for it. He adds "I would go down to pinpoint it from the point of view of the realities. We must face these realities. The realities are that in the last few years there has been enormous proliferation of the areas in which Government has started its functioning. Enormous proliferation is there because somehow or other the functionaries of the Government have gone on expanding their activities not because they want to do so but because of the inevitability of the operations of administrative progression of the country. They have necessitated a proliferation of the laws and the extreme proliferation of the rules and the procedures relating to the implementation of those laws. On account of this proliferation, it has become absolutely impossible for even a smallest functionary to operate rightly or expeditiously on any problem. Even though he may be honest. Let us assume that a functionary at the lower level i.e. a Clerk, an Asstt. or a Superintendent, is honest and he wants to help. Can he? No! Let us assume, for the purpose of discussion, that he wants to help. But there are rules, there are procedures, there are forms and on the bases of these forms and procedures, even if they are convinced of the genuineness of a case they cannot operate because if there would be something lacking then the inadequacy ultimately would reflect on their career. Their career will be blasted by that. They know that they will be held responsible for not functioning on these bases and, therefore, they will delay it. Secondly, for a dishonest person it brings a great opportunity for riding over and telling a citizen... that 'you do it this way then we will do the work'. These are few things for which we must, as I say, have to get to micro level. Only then we will understand the problems which are being experienced. It would lead us to find better solutions''.

H.S. Anand belonging to Indian Administraive Service, has a doctorate in Sociology to his credit. Besides serving at the District and Sub-Division levels, he is presently Director, Ministry of Urban Development, Government of India. He has presented a picture of the present administration thus:

''The Indian administrative system is based on the steelframe of the ICS, which was left to us as a legacy. The Indian Administrative Service has been structured broadly on generalist-specialist pattern. This system has its main strength in that the incumbents or the members of the service get extensive training at the field level as Sub-Divisional Magistrates and later as Additional Deputy Commissioners and, finally, as District Magistrates. This experience where they are in touch with the various aspects of the administrative life and they are co-ordinating the work of almost all the departments at the field level brings them very close to the common man. The common man is free to meet the Deputy Commissioner at specified times with any form of complaint or any form of grievance that he may have. There is also in the district, in most states of the country, a complaints and inquiry branch which has specifically been designed to make the administration more responsive to the public and any person can give a complaint which would then be registered and, in an appropriate time, he can re-enquire as to what has happened to his complaint. In many states, there is also the system of monthly meeting, which is normally chaired by either a cabinet member of the state government or a senior MLA, and a number of local public persons from various parties as well as some social workers and other eminent citizens are also associated with this meeting. During this meeting, not only certain complaints made by the public are discussed but also the action taken by the administration is brought to light. The complainants themselves are invited to be present and then the complainants can raise supplementaries in response to the action taken. This is another mechanism by which the administration seeks to be more responsive. Besides this, in many states, the District Magistrates and Sub-Divisional Magistrates have also been asked to have an open Darbar from time to time for listening to the grievances of the people on the spot.

"Now, while I have painted a reasonably structured system that is available for the redressal of the grievances, it is a fact that still quite a few grievances either go unanswered or the common man still has a perceived sense of hurt that redressal takes too long and is too cumbersome. I would think that this is partly true and this is true because the quantum of work that devolves on the District Magistrate or the Secretaries or on officers working in various Ministries, is very substantial. During the British days, the administration was largely restricted to regulatory functions and there were only a few developmental functions to be performed. The volume of developmental functions has grown substantially after independence. The regulation also has varied aspects given the fact that the country does from time to time come up with problems of communal harmony, problems of border states, and problems of terrorism, which throw up their own genre of demands impinging heavily on the time of the civil service. Also the Indian bureaucratic system is structured on a very long hierarchy between the lowest and the highest functionaries. This causes delay in responding to the problems and grievances of the people. Moreover, at times, the functionaries at the lower levels are not all that straight. All these aspects combined certainly stand in the way of functioning of administration in a speedy and effective manner and also create problems for the administration to be as responsive as aspired for".

Understanding, realizing and in a way admitting also that the man at the railway counter is not all that honest, R.D. Kitson, Chairman, Railway Board, feels proud of the administrative system of the Indian Railways. He puts it in his own words thus:

"We have very vast set of administrators, officers, managers, and superintendents. This system is so intensively complicated on one hand and so simple on the other. I am very happy to say, as far as administrative responsiveness is concerned, that it is total and complete. There are areas of weaknesses which we must accept in the large organisations like that of ours. But the system is very firm and very solid. Over a period of time, we have refined those areas where there were weaknesses. We hope that we will be better and better in the times to come. We know what ought to be done and how it should be done. When you come down to the ground you come across an altogether different set of circumstances. I must say that our people who have interface with the public are intelligent and knowledgeable but they are surrounded by the unfortunate aspect of the demand of the day which is much greater than the supply. Under these circumstances they are generally being harassed by the public and they themselves are also harassing the public. It is both ways.

"I have to admit that the character and culture of the average Indian has changed over a period of time. In fact, I think we have to redefine what corruption is and what does it mean? The number of people travelling everyday in the country has gone considerably up. We are still far short of meeting with the requirements. The demand is more and the supply in correspondence to that is less. Because of this and also due to the loose character in the terms of moral standards, the travelling public adopt underhand means which our railway men are there to take with open hands. I am not saying that there are many of them but there are.

"You get first major breakdown in the system in which the honest are not protected and the dishonest get a reward, it affects and affects heavily the morale and motivation of the honest lot. What we are doing is to bring behavioural and attitudinal changes among the thinking of our workforce through seminars, workshops and cultural organisations. The field officials are the ones who are being seen by the public who come in contact with the people, these field officials include booking clerk, parcel clerk, ticket collector, station master, etc. People see them and not us in the Board. We interact with the public only when we are in trains or at the platforms. We are, therefore, trying our best to train the field staff. We are trying to induct railwaymen's children at the young age of 12-13 years into the railway system, trying to educate and prepare them for the railways at this very young age when they are not having corrupt minds. We would then be putting these well trained young people into the field to perform the jobs in a better manner.

Until that happens the problems would be there but the question really is that everybody must respond and not only the railwaymen''.

Formerly Comptroller and Auditor General of India, T.N. Chaturvedi, having an illustrious service record at different higher rungs of the administration, has viewed the issue of administrative responsiveness with a philosophical and conceptual viewpoint. He says that it is very difficult to measure, evaluate or quantify the administrative responsiveness. It has to be taken into account on the basis of the extent of satisfaction or dissatisfaction of the people and one of the measures or yardsticks to evaluate it could be the image or perception of the individuals coming in contact with different parts of the administration. He opined:

''Administration is not just monolithic, it has to be segmental. Though there is always unity of corporate approach and understanding behind it, yet each group has a different set of requirements and problems so it is said to be segmental. It does not mean just the fragmentation of administration but the question is of limited interest or contact of one group with the relevant sector of the administration. If I have to go by the city transport bus every morning then how do I perceive the problems relating to that. I will have different capacity and different ways of coming into contact with the administration. I would cease to be an administrator in this situation. If I am in administration, entrusted with the responsibility, then how do I react to these problems. This is the way, I think, we can look into the problems''.

He feels that by and large, the expectations of the people from the relevant segments of administration they come in contact with are not being fulfilled. ''There is some kind of disenchantment amongst the people, some disillusionment regarding their expectations. Probably they expect much more. Whether it may be segmentally looked at or being looked at in the totality of the administration, both ways it is the same. The responsiveness of administration has to be in conformity with the expectations of the people, in conformity with what they aspire and what they get''.

Chaturvedi says that there is enormous increase in the expectations of the people. ''This is generated due to populist politics which may not be supported by the resources, the proper strategies, the proper policies and the continuity of policies in an adequate way. There may be a little bit of political chicanery involved in it''.

Another reason for the lack of responsiveness, he feels, is lack of understanding between the citizens and the administrators. ''Every administrator is a citizen and an administrator. Why talk of the stereotype of administrative officer alone, take a doctor, a teacher, an advocate, a railway booking clerk, anybody who has some authority, must not forget that he is to use the authority for the benefit of others. When one is holding authority he just forgets that at times he may have to go to others also for some work and even if not so he must attempt to stand in the shoes of the person approaching him and should do the job. There is a split in the personality of a democratic citizen. There is need to do away with this kind of the split. This is the only way to evoke response from both sides of the so called public participation, public cooperation and so on''.

T.N. Chaturvedi is of the opinion that ''the administrative response is not a sloganised statement, it is not a platitude. It is a very exerting process. It has to suffuse the entire attitude of the administration, of the political leadership of the citizens and of the total society. Administration is not isolated from the entire social set-up. There are a number of qualities, requirements, or attributes which are required to go alongwith it''.

V.C. Kulandai Swamy, an eminent educationist having vast intellectual potentialities and rich administrative experience of managing different universities for a long time feels that among the innumerable deficiencies and weaknesses which are there in the Indian system, the most important one is the weakness of the administrative system of India. The prime and basic philosophy behind the system of administration in India is not up to the mark. He puts it thus: ''Often people find out deficiencies with regard to the policies, with regard to the contents of different policies. Hardly people touch upon the fact that it is the administrative system which plays more negative role so far as the ultimate failure of these policies is concerned. The one aspect that needs to be attended to rather urgently is our administrative system''.

He does not think that there is anything known as pure and simple administration. In his opinion, ''Administration is not something that is divorced from the knowledge of the subject field that is being administered. Administration is a component, it is something like a salt for a food, salt by itself does not become food. So the very first weakness in our administrative system is that it is under the charge of people who may or may not have any knowledge of the department or the subject being administered''.

Police is meant to maintain peace, law and order. Every citizen, rich or poor, young or old, strives for it throughout his life and at all the places. Keeping in view the importance, significance and role of police in present day's society, we interviewed two very senior police officers and in order to have continuity in the presentation of their viewpoints to our queries, we are deviating a bit from the alphabetical order while analysing their perceptions.

Arun Bhagat, a senior officer belonging to the Indian Police Service, who was Police Commissioner of Delhi when we interviewed him, felt that in cases of urgency the police force was thoroughly responsive. When asked to give his perception of responsiveness on the part of police especially keeping in view the feelings of the common man that when he approaches the police he is not being heard properly and the police does not take quick action, Arun Bhagat stated : "I do not think it is possible to make any generalisations or come to any general conclusion. There are instances of a very very quick and prompt response and, of course, there are times also when there are delays. Responsiveness on the part of police would be of different nature. I mean different requirements are there. For example, the police control room response is always very good and our police control room vehicles reach the spot of trouble or accident within 3 to 5 minutes. This I think is a very good response time. Now as regards response from the police station that would also depend on the nature of the problem which is posed to them: if they are told there has been a robbery, a dacoity or a murder or somebody has been injured or there is a riot, the response is extremely quick. But, if it is a question of theft having taken place from a car or in a building then even if there is a little bit of delay, I do not think it is very material. So the responses would be dependent upon the nature of the call, the nature of the problem which has been there. Certainly, there is lot of need for more improvement of police responses, its nature of interaction with the public, and also for increasing the helpfulness on the part of police personnel. Specific training programmes have been initiated by the police departments not only in Delhi but throughout the country. There could be instances of police harassment and corrupt dealings but these are only exceptions rather than rule".

Another senior police officer approached was Vijay Karan, then Director, Central Bureau of Investigation. He honestly admitted that police did not have a positive image and lot more was required to be done for increasing its credibility and acceptability in the society. He stated: "The police force all over country has a very bad image. It is not at all responsive, it is regarded as negative, it is regarded as corrupt and it is regarded as high-handed and that is not only the image of the police in India but that has been the behaviour pattern of police all through and this has to be changed. My view is that a police organisation is a service-oriented organisation. It is there and it has been created for the sake of serving the people, protecting the people, looking after them, and maintaining law and order. Seeing that society is free from criminal activities, the police force role has no other alternative but to be responsive to the needs and requirements of the people and also their grievances. That is why when I was the Commissioner of Police, I tried to bring about change in the overall ethos, behaviour and culture of the police. I wanted the police to respond to the people not only to protect them and maintain law and order but to look upon the people as an entity and whose grievances count a lot. I mean that is why, for instance, I tried to eliminate third degree method altogether also. It is our job to serve the people, we have no right to beat up the people. If a policeman beats the criminal today to extract confession, tomorrow the same policeman will not hesitate to beat up a citizen also or even beat up an innocent person who might be suspected of having committed an offence but who might be still an innocent. I am very strongly of the view that police has to be responsive towards the citizen''.

III (a) Politicians' Perceptions of Political Leaders' Interference in Administration

Whenever one talks to the administrative officials to know about the reasons for their low performance leading to the lack of responsiveness of the administration, by and large, the response is that there is considerable amount of pressure from the political functionaries and the leaders as a result of which it becomes difficult for the administration to take up its tasks properly.

Harkishan Singh Surjeet opined that the top leadership had to improve a lot because looking at it the functionaries at the lower levels work in wrong directions. He did not go exactly alongwith the view that administration was lethargic because of political pressures but said that the administration was in connivance with the political functionaries in committing wrongs. In his words: ''This is a corollary of what is happening at the top. How people make so much of money and properties? After doing all this even the top leaders and the Ministers cannot control or check the lower level ranks. The people at the grassroots also try to use the same methods and pressures. But the pressure of this kind is used only by those who have got some levers of power in their hands. I would say that if the administration starts looking at the problem from the angle of interest of mass of the people the problem of political interference would automatically get minimised. What administrators are doing is moving slowly on each and every thing and eating money as a result of which the deterioration in the administrative functioning is on the substantive increase. They don't do it alone but the political forces are patronising it and the share of the booty goes everywhere. I will not say that all are like that but it is a general phenomenon. It is very difficult to find out a good, honest, and efficient administrator and similarly, one has to find out that such and such persons even at the top political level also are honest. The political leaders and functionaries who try to influence upon the administrators for their own ends may get some immediate benefits out of it but ultimately they would be at a loss because doing so they are only destroying the very fabric of this country. A consciousness to this effect has to be created for not encouraging these ill-designs. For that the remedial measure could be that the administration puts to an end the favours being granted to only few for winning over the political leaders and the political leaders should try their best not to corrupt the administration and through it and them the system''.

After knowing Harkishan Singh Surjeet's above mentioned views, two questions were put to him. Firstly, would he blame the citizens also for making political leaders influence the administrators?; and secondly, does he feel that in West Bengal, where presently the CPM is running the government, one has these problems or not? His views regarding the first question were:

''Citizens also are to be blamed because as I said degeneration has set in a big way. The self-interest has become more predominant rather than the interest of the community and the nation. Everybody says, 'let me get my job done and why bother about others'. I will tell you one such example. A person whom I have known for the last thirty years and who besides being a party worker is our family friend also approached me for helping him to be the village Numberdar. I frankly told him that I won't help him on this count. He has approached some other leader and has got his work done. Because I did not help him he is thoroughly annoyed with me now. For him being Numberdar was too big a thing. Now once he has got it through the help of someone, we could easily make out what would be his style of functioning. So I say that the citizens should also not be that over ambitious for getting wrong and undeserving things and benefits. They must cooperate with the administration''.

To our second question regarding conditions prevailing in West Bengal, Harkishan Singh Surjeet stated:

''There is some check. I will not say nothing of this sort is happening there. These things are operating there as well but at the political level such things are not there. If we find something of this sort at political level, we take immediate action against the party functionary may even he be a Minister. So that is comparatively better. We have adopted some measures like decentralising the administration, expenditure meant for development works handed over to the Panchayats, political check but not interference on the administration etc. Still, I don't say that it is totally free from all vices. We are seized of it and are taking measures for further improvement''.

Surjeet further said that the political institutions at the grassroots must be strengthened as it is these institutions and bodies, in his view, which could provide not only a healthy check on the administration but also on those selfish political leaders who join hands with the administration and add to the negativities and deterioration.

Administrative functionaries' ways of performance amount to the political interference in their domain. Indrajit Gupta strongly holds this opinion and states, ''Administrators' own bureaucratic perceptions and behaviour are often reinforced by the subjective interference of some politicians. This may be the fall-out of growing criminalization of the election process and the compulsions of casteism and communalisation, etc. But all political leaders should not be tarred with the same brush''.

Indrajit Gupta favours decentralisation of administration and says that decentralising of the administrative powers is a must for expecting better performance of the administration. In his words, ''Panchayati Raj is essential''. Besides strengthening of Panchayati Raj in a real meaningful manner, he is of the view that the ''political parties must eschew the use of money power and muscle power for getting votes''.

K.C. Pant strongly feels that the point made by the administrative functionaries regarding interference of political leaders does not hold much ground as the political leaders are answerable to people and so are more sensitive to their problems. Simultaneously, he has referred to norms and standards to be adopted by political leaders as well. In his own words he puts it thus, "Among the political leaders and administrators good and bad elements are there. The politicians are generally closer to various problems of the people. They are elected by the people and, therefore, have to be responsive to the desires and prevalent moods and feelings of the people. They also have to make sure that the wants and feelings of the people are fulfilled".

Pant further said: "There are distortions like booth capturing, etc. I would not like to go into that, but, by and large, this is true and one of the problems is that the kind of people who are coming to the political system, who get elected, and who become ministers have to be made aware of the need to go by norms, standards and avoid discretionary action or decisions. This is one part of it and on the other side, the administrators have to understand the pressures under which the politicians work and they have to understand that anyone who has to seek elections has some pressures working on him. This is true of all democracies. Therefore, a working system has to be evolved which is, by and large, fair, just and proceeds according to the law and which at the same time takes care of the realities on the ground.

"Now, if there is a tendency on the part of government officers to always be suspicious about the politicians then also the system does not work and if the politician always seeks to disregard the sound advice of the administrators even though he is disinterested at times and particularly when he punishes him that also makes the system somewhat vulnerable. So, we are passing through a phase during which we have the politics going up and newer sections and elements of political leaders are coming to power, therefore, a constant process of learning the basic principles of administration is required. I think the need is to view the democracy functioning not only effectively but also the distortions that seem to be setting in with the greater use of money and muscle power have to be kept in mind for evolving a sound mechanism of functioning in a manner which suits the interests of the commoners.

"We can hope to arrive at the right equilibrium. It is not the question of blaming one or the other, it is the question of everybody understanding his role and the role is not adversarial. It is complementary. I want to further add that the political leadership is answerable and goes to people with a manifesto for elections. In a democracy, the word and policy of the politician must prevail and there should be no grumbling or no questions on it. Other things are mechanical part of it but I am referring to them because they also have significance. But I do not want confusion on the basic structure of our polity. The basic role of a politician and an administrator is getting benefits to the public at large''.

L.K. Advani views the basic lowering down of values and standards as adversely affecting the politicians and administrators functioning and believes it to be a major cause of breakdown in the system. He also strongly feels concerned about the negative and parochial attitude of both the political leaders and the administrators regarding transfers of the administrators. The handle of transfers, which the political leaders in power have, is often being considered as a sword hanging over the heads of the administrative functionaries and often they attempt to please the political bosses by doing wrong acts at their behest. Advani stated it thus:

''I would say that when there is deterioration in values, in abilities and in commitments in the total society, the deterioration is bound to be in the politicians and administrators. The tendency now is to look for scapegoats. The politicians blame the bureaucrats, the bureaucrats blame the politicians, both together they blame the people and the people blame everyone else. This is what is going on. The fact is that everyone is contributing to the present mess and so I have always advised whosoever meets me or whosoever I can influence that in such a situation, one has to be scrupulous about his own self and should influence whosoever he can to this effect. There are no other solutions and I do not think either this or that is wholly to blame. For example, on the issue of transfers, I am to say that it is a very peculiar aspect, there are party activists and party supporters who come to me and say that in this particular case, this transfer has been ordered, and this must be stopped. When I try to make them understand that this is not the right way of going about, then they say 'if this small work cannot be done then what could be done? We have been working in this party for so long?; we have been supporting this party day after day, election after election and, of course, so long as you were in the opposition it was alright but now that you are in power and you cannot do even such simple and small problems then what benefit do we get out of it?' It looks too small to them but it has major repercussions on the system.

''I always try to convince people who approach me for such work. The BJP has governments in four states now and one of the major problems before them is how to deal with transfer issues? I often tell my colleagues in these states about this. I can understand this thing that in case of the government officers in 95 per cent of cases where an Officer is transferred from one place to another, there are bound to be some kind of family dislocations. It will be only 5 per cent cases where a transfer does not mean dislocation of any kind. I am sure that out of those 95 per cent at least 80 per cent must be knowing some MLA, some MP, some party worker, some so and so, and out of those 80 per cent, some 50 per cent may be knowing me personally. So after all if Advani says how can it not be done? They come and tell me, 'you see, my mother is very old; she is ailing and my children are still in school; it is a very genuine case.' Everyone who comes to me says his is a very genuine case. 'I am not pleading for any promotion. I am not pleading for anything wrong'. I have to explain to every such person that 95 per cent of cases of his kind are genuine in human terms but at the same time if out of these 95 per cent, 70 per cent transfers are to be stopped because of political influence, then Government cannot function. At least, I am not going to be a party to it because using political influence for transfers or using it as a threat to the administrators affects the administrative functioning very badly. I would also say that neither the administrators should strive for it nor the politicians and both should work in accordance with the best of administrative principles, norms, standards, and constraints of each other''.

Ram Jethmalani has views different from others on the issue of political interference in the administration. He feels that political leaders and functionaries are responsible for the deterioration which has come up in the administrative system. He further holds the view that citizen must be educated to understand and appreciate the total process fairly well and not to run after the political leaders for getting him his due also as a favour. He put it thus:

''Political leaders and functionaries are wholly responsible for it and are certainly exaggerating the problem by their own conduct and behaviour. Today, are the politicians serious and responsible for the people's need? No, they are always busy feathering their own nests all the time and today why do people enter politics? They enter politics because it provides them power and the power provides them perks and opportunities for corruption and getting rich. You look around, who has become rich except politicians, leave aside a few distinguished professionals who have become rich. It is the bad influence of politicians which has ruined the administration. You cannot make a start at the grassroots, as they say, you have to start with the top. You must purify the Gangotri because the poison in the Gangotri is seeping down to every village, every river, every canal, so one has to start from the top.

"The common man, if intelligently exercises his voting power and votes for such people who are knwon for selfless service and integrity and character, there is a way out to be away from the clutches of politicians and administrators who for their own ends exploit the citizens. There must be proper education of the people. Unless complete information about how our politicians are behaving?; what is their character?; what is their conduct?; and, the manner in which they are sort of stealing the poor man's wealth reaches the poor people, they cannot form accurate judgement. The dissemination of information is in the hands of very corrupt people whose interest it is to hide it for the sake of hiding their corrupt means. So the poor man is at a terrible disadvantage. Though some newspapers are doing this job, yet how many people read newspapers. The newspapers do not percolate down to the people. So I am afraid it is a very very grave long range problem.

"There is need to educate people. Those who have the perception of what is happening in the country?; how the politicians have literally cheated in this country?; etc., must pick up sufficient courage to tell all others. Unfortunately, the intellecturals have also failed in their duties in the country. They are too busy with the problems of their own survival and take a line of least resistance. I strongly believe that political functionaries are responsible to a much considerable extent for all the problems because they have the ultimate power. The common man must keep a vigilant eye on the operations of these politicians who are in power and weave them out, expose them, and criticize them. He should act bravely in this matter. The common citizen must know his rights. There is need to put some steel in his backbone so that he also stands to the insolence of the power".

Keeping in view the basic profession of Ram Jethmalani, he was asked to comment on the fact that if the common man does not get justice or whatever is his due he goes to the court of law and there also it takes him too long to get justice, if at all he gets it. Jethmalani replied: "You see, a corrupt politician or a man who is in power, if he is corrupt the first thing that he needs is the corrupt judges. So the character of the appointing authority gets reflected in the character of those who are appointed. So that is what has happened to the judiciary. But, let me be very clear that I still think that comparing to the other departments of public life, our judiciary is still the best. They have been working under great temptation, great pressures and all that. There are a few good ones. The good ones are so good that they almost redeem the reputation and character of the whole family. But I can say that our judiciary provides no actual relief to the common man''.

Subramaniam Swamy feels that political interference is there, rather more at the lower levels. The political functionaries behave in an unethical manner and due to lack of courage, strength and unwanted fear alongwith their own wrong acts, the administrative functionaries fall prey to this. He said:

''The problem at the grassroots level is that the ruling party worker thinks that he owns the government or he is the master. He further believes that the lower level functionaries -- the Police Thanedar or any official -- have to work as he says and so on. He often makes them do wrong work and when the party he belongs to goes out of power, and the other set of his fellow beings come they take revenge on these things. This amounts to the whole process of transfers. The political functionaries instead of interfering in the day-to-day work of the administration serving their own interests should rather fight against injustices of the administration on principles. Keeping in view the frequent changes in the governments it becomes all the more necessary to keep the administration politically neutral for getting benefits to all. Citizen's committees comprising representatives of all political parties at the grassroots should be formed and these should take up the issues with the administration not on individual but on objective basis and should interact with the government officials rather than interfering every now and then for each and every thing. By all means, political neutrality of the administration has to be ensured, maintained, and preserved''.

Yashwant Sinha feels that both the politicians and administrators have not been able to understand and appreciate the role of each other. In his opinion this is the major reason for the kind of blame on each other; as per political leaders the administrators are not working properly and the administrators feel that political leaders are interfering in their work. Sinha observes it as ''a two way traffic''.

''The politicians, if one talks to them would say that administration is very callous and not responsive at all. I think the basic problem in our polity has been that the administration on the one hand and the politician on the other have not so far learnt to co-exist, because norms of conduct have not been defined on either side. How exactly the two shall conduct the affairs of the public has been left to chances, therefore, lot of problems arise again because of the personality factor. But the administrators or the bureaucrats who complain that because of the politicians or due to political interference they have not been able to perform their the duties are not all that right. You see, you go to any government office which deals with people, take a block development officer or any development department for that matter or police station or excise and taxation or anything else, you will find a large crowd of people in those offices all the time and most of them will complain that they have not been able to talk or they have not been listened to, they have not been treated as human beings, they have not been shown any courtesy and day after day they go to offices and come. When I was in the administration, I had devised my own law. I used to call it law of diminishing courtesy. There is a law of diminishing courtesy which operates. What happens is that if you seek an appointment and you get it with a senior officer then he will receive you and ask you to sit down and talk to you about your problems. But when you start going down and down, you meet more and more callousness and this is something which I noticed myself even as an officer. I sought an appointment with somebody; he said, 'alright now this work will be done'; ultimately in order to expedite the work, I had to go and meet the functionary at the lowest rung and the functionary at the lowest rung was the most discourteous''.

III (b) Political Leaders' Perceptions of Training of Political Leaders

Politicians and administrators both have a major role to perform in providing and maintaining the most viable system of administration whereby not only the regulatory and development tasks are performed better but are performed to the benefit, satisfaction and to the expectations of the citizens. Somehow or the other, with passage of time, an unfortunate situation has emerged wherein both these performers have developed a feeling of mistrust for each other and each is blaming the other. Most of the problems on account of so called interference by political leaders in the daily tasks of administration, as felt seriously by sizeable number of administrators and some of the right thinking politicians also, is due to the fact that the political leaders do not understand and appreciate theirs as well as administrators' roles, priorities, privileges, and compulsions.

Yashwant Sinha feels that the training of political leaders can do a lot but simultaneously he is of the view that the administrative functionaries should be put to thorough training for bringing an overall change in their working pattern and behaviour. He opined:

"The important thing is for each segment to understand clearly what is the role and responsibility of the other segment. I can appreciate the stand taken by an administrator only when I know the role and compulsions of the functionary who is to carry out the work. This point could be brought home with the political representatives through specially conducted training programmes and orientation camps. I tell you the elected representatives are limited in number but people in politics and in public life are a large segment. I am referring not only to the political leaders but also to the vast number of do gooders through NGOs and other voluntary organisations who are trying to help people. What response from the administration they are getting? It is a very dismaying scene. I believe that anybody who is trying to act as a bridge between the citizens and the administration should be encouraged to do so. These people operate in local areas, they understand the problems and grievances of the public of that area, the administration should listen to them and sort out the grievances brought to its notice by them. This change in the working and attitude of administrators is a must.

"I have been at the receiving end and at the giving end both. I will tell you that my experience at the receiving end has not been very encouraging. As a former bureaucrat I have no hesitation in saying that I felt extremely disappointed and defeated at times at the kind of response I had received from the bureaucracy. In a nutshell, I am strongly of the view that the orientation and training for political leaders is essential and also essential is the training for civil servants".

K.C. Pant admits that there are a number of instances when the political leaders pressurise the administrative functionaries to help the individuals they are interested in. At times these political leaders interfere in the administration also and want that the work they have asked for must be accomplished immediately. They don't understand the pressure of work and constraints of the administrators. Pant's observations with regard to starting training for political leaders were:

"There are instances when the political leaders behave in an uncalled for manner and pressurise the administration for doing wrongs. As I said earlier it is not the question of blaming one or the other. One should think seriously for evolving the right kind of attitudes and approach. And in fact, sometimes, I think that in USA they have the Keneddy School of Government in which the newly elected politicians at all levels from local to the higher get training. They interact with young government officers and this interaction, I am told, helps to define the role of each and leads to a much better understanding of each other's role and much better cooperation between the political leaders and the administrators. I sometimes wonder if it is not a desirable step to be taken in our country also''.

Pant further said: ''It is not necessary, not just, only to expose the administrators to a course of training which prepares them for their work. But it is equally necessary to train political representatives. It is perhaps necessary to have interaction between the administrators and the elected representatives for better understanding. In India, we started one week courses of this kind at Administrative Staff College of India at Hyderabad, but may be one requires longer courses. What is required is a more concentrated effort with exposure to various aspects of administrative functioning. I attended one of those courses at ASCI and I did not find it to be bad at all. I can speak for myself, I got more out of it than I had expected. The structure of the course was designed to lead to a better understanding of the decision making processes which I thought was useful. What I have in mind is not these one week courses but somewhat longer in the shape of integrated modules taken up in a serious manner, where you talk of the Constitution, few important ideas about the role of the administrator and an effort to understand the pressures of work on both alongwith the limits and obligations of both''.

L.K. Advani when asked to comment on this issue, was of the view that his party had been taking this aspect seriously. After coming to power in four states they were paying greater attention to this aspect. He believed that such type of training would go a long way in making the political functionaries appreciate the complexities of the administrative system, its procedures and rules. He stated:

''We in our party actually keep on organising camps in which the political leaders are told about the administrative procedures and practices. This facet has been added recently in our training activities. Earlier we used to have focus mainly on organisational policies and work of our party. But lately after the BJP has come into office in several governments, the political leaders are sensitised to the administrative functioning and administrators' obligations for ensuring smooth sailing of the system. Though we have been attempting to educate and train our cadres to this effect, yet as such the results are not that fruitful. I am sure after few years it would show its positive colours''.

Subramaniam Swamy does not feel that training for politicians could be of any help. He does not find the training culture prevalent in India, especially with the political functionaries. He rather believes that society must make a climate whereby politics is considered as a challenging profession. He firmly said:

''Training for political leaders cannot do much good. I think what we need is that society should create a climate where the educated people and the qualified people go into politics. You cannot train politicians, it is impossible. The work pressures on them are such, incentive is very little and above all who is going to impart training to them. For instance, there are computer courses for members of Parliament every session, just you go and see how many MPs are going to learn that. So the only way is that the society which has created the climate so far in India is of the kind that only the corrupt go into politics and the decent people go into professions, this must change. Politics must also be regarded as a challenging profession in which good and educated people should go. That is the only way, I don't think there is going to be much benefit with the training''. Ram Jethmalani was asked to comment on the issue. His reply was ''Well, you might start a school for S.......That might improve the administration''. Though he commented jokingly about it probably without meaning much about the word used, which, even though he is a Parliamentarian himself, is rather unparliamentarian to make use of. But he felt that such training could help.

IV Administrators' Perceptions of Political Leaders' Interference in Administration

The politicians have desire for power, patronage, and money. Over the years, mainly because of these ends of theirs, the political leaders have started behaving unethically with the administration. On the basis of his experiences, B.B. Vohra quotes an example from earlier days that makes clear why and how the political leaders behave so now, and what is the possible way to come out of it. He said:

"I think that things have changed very much during the last 35 years or so. When I was Deputy Commissioner, there was political pressure even then but the politician was not yet bold enough to ride roughshod over the opinion given to him or the advice given to him by the administrator. For example, I remember very well that when Mr. P.S. Kairon became the Chief Minister, Punjab, very soon afterwards he transferred two of my magistrates by telegram without a word of consultation with me. Of course, the orders came from the Home Secretary and when I rang him up to ask why it has been done, the tenure of these officers is by no means over, he said that these were the Chief Minister's orders. I said I would like to meet the Chief Minister. I was given permission to do so, those days permission was required for a Deputy Commissioner to meet the Chief Minister. I got the permission, motored down to Chandigarh and met Mr. Kairon. I asked him why he had taken this step, as in my opinion these officers were excellent officers, who were doing their duty in a very conscientious way. He said, 'oh! I have received complaints against them and this is my decision'. I then said, 'Sardar Saheb in that case I shall be proceeding on leave and I feel I will not be able to discharge my responsibilities as the District Magistrate in the new circumstances and I hope you will be able to give me leave immediately and then replace me.' When I said this, he immediately relented, changed his tune and said, 'no, no, no, you misunderstood me, this is nothing and if you feel so I withdraw the orders. You go back and work with boldness'. I was surprised, pleasantly surprised, but he was good enough to take back those orders immediately and I went back as a very satisfied officer. Looking back over this event, I feel that it will be impossible now for such a thing to happen because the politician is no longer diffident so to say. There were good traditions at that time. But today it is entirely different".

Vohra feels that the politician wants to have an administration which supports him in his designs. In his words, "You see, in India, the kind of democracy we have, it demands that the politician must have access to patronage, he also must have access to a great deal of ready cash in order to discharge his obligations towards his supporters. So this means that the administration must be flexible enough to satisfy the demands of the politicians, so it is matter of survival for the politicians and under the present system we cannot really afford to have the rule of law to coexist with the demands of the politicians. So, over the years, the politicians have seen to it that the back of administrators is broken by various easy devices such as frequent transfers or keeping them on the sideline, not preferring straightforward and strong officers. Such strong officers were marginalised and other people came up and this gave the message that this is the new type of officers needed and demand follows supply. I think this is what has happened. The officers also can not be expected to be heroes or martyrs or saints, they have to cope with the demands of daily life, education of their children, family circumstances and so on. They got demoralised, so, by and large, they have fallen in line with the politicians' whims''.

As per B.B. Vohra the ray of hope to come out of this situation is that, ''The ordinary people are more or less beginning to appreciate that they can get justice only if the administration is non-political. And I think as this realisation spreads and grows they are bound to demand change in the existing arrangements. People are becoming more conscious of their rights, more politically conscious, there is also a strong press, the opposition parties also feel that the parliamentary democracy can function effectively only if there is an independent, neutral, non-political administration. Somehow, we have to harmonise this with the love of the politicians for patronage and power and money. This is a real problem before us''.

Commenting on the politicians-administrators relationship, while emphasising on the need for training for political leaders, H.D. Shourie holds the view that the politicians do not appreciate the rules, regulations and constraints of the administrators. They want the officials to toe their lines or face consequences, like transfers. While making his point, Shourie also mentioned about the relationship between the politicians and administrators in the early years of independence. In his words, ''Increasingly, I have developed the view that the most unfortunate development that has gone in the country is the relationship between the bureaucrats and the politicians. It has developed to an extent which is hampering in reaching out of administration to people. Let me put it this way. A minister of the Punjab Government was to visit Rohtak, where I was Deputy Commissioner. I received a telephonic call from the then Chief Secretary that the Minister would be reaching Rohtak in the evening at about 9 O'clock and I should meet him. I said, certainly I will meet him. And at about 9 O'Clock, I knew that the minister would come to a certain place, so I went there to meet him. I was told that the minister had reached. Was on the upper floor. There was open area and there he was sitting on the roof. I went there. I found about 15 to 20 people surrounding the minister. They were of Rohtak where I was the Deputy Commissioner. I said to the minister, 'Good evening, Sir, I have come, I am the Deputy Commissioner, Rohtak'. He said, 'wait, I am busy'. I said 'where should I wait, downstairs in the car or here on the roof'. He did not reply to that. I went down and instead of waiting told the attendant to convey to the minister that the Deputy Commissioner of Rohtak came and has gone away and he would not be able to come again. I conveyed this to the then Chief Minister that this is what has happened, I was belittled deliberately in the presence of those 15, 20 persons of Rohtak. It would become extremely detrimental, my effectiveness would be affected. I said 'in these circumstances I have considered necessary to inform you of what has happened and how the minister behaved'. The Chief Minister supported me. Well, that was that time when it could happen and this cannot happen now.

"Unfortunately, the type of ministers, the type of politicians that have come into the picture now are those who have spoiled the atmosphere. Some of them are illiterate, some of them have record which can only be described as that of criminals. These people have vitiated the total surroundings. With regard to the officers, I am sure that majority of the people in the administration at the senior levels are motivated by proper desire of rendering the service and, of course, they have to look at their career from the point of view of going ahead in life by doing the proper job and that is the proper thing to do. There is nothing wrong in looking ahead for the development of one's interests. But, unfortunately, the politician now because of his, I can say, complusions but at the same time also due to his personal requirements, wants to get things done through the officer under pressure and threat, with the result, that the officers have started also cowing down before the politicans and this is very bad. The politicians must be sensitised to their as well as officials' role and obligations. They must be prepared to pursue their task effectively and to let the administration perform in the best manner. There should be detailed programmes for them to this an effect".

Shourie further said: "In this context, the areas of operations of a politician need to be reduced from the point of veiw of his interaction with the officers. The transfer can be effected of any official from one place to another at the wills and requirements of the politician. That is where the whole rough lies. The politician ultises this handle. For avoiding it the governance must work out a formula whereby the transfers could be monitored. It would provide ample courage, strength and opportunity to the administrators for proving their worth''.

In a democratic polity, political leadership and political parties ought to be more vigilant about the needs, demands, and expectations of the people because they survive on that only. In such a system the key role is that of the political leaders and institutions, more so at the lower levels, than that of the administration. G. Ram Reddy has his views altogether different than that of a number of politicians and administrators with regard to the issue of interference of politicians in the day-to-day administration. He firmly said, ''That is what bureaucracy would feel. They don't want any interference from outside, but left to themselves they would not be able to deliver the goods. There has to be somebody who will tell them, from time-to-time, what is to be done and how it is to be done. So accountability of the administration is ensured through the political masters. In a democracy, you cannot wish away the political element, it is the job of the political masters to ensure responsiveness in administration. Well, in the case of politically elected bodies they are responsible to the people. Sometimes they could also be indifferent, but they have to fight an election every five years and the bureaucracy has no election to fight. Therefore, bureaucracy can afford to be callous, very slow and indifferent. But the politicians, on the other hand, cannot afford to be indifferent, they may sometimes indulge in excesses but certainly they are more responsive to the people's needs''.

Politics and administration cannot be viewed as absolutely distinct entities independent of each other. Both have to work unitedly. The politicians have to be more responsive to the citizens' needs and wants. Simultaneously, there has to be a well defined procedure for writing of the confidential roles of the senior civil servants and the issue of transfers, etc., must be tackled with more seriousness. H.S. Anand talked about some of these points while referring to the issue of interference in the administration by the political leaders. He said:

''It would be false to look at the administration as something which is divorced from politics. It would be incorrect to look at the higher administrative structure in isolation with the political structure. In a country which has adopted a democratic system of government, the elected representatives of the people and especially the party in power and the people in the cabinet, have direct responsibility for realising in practice the electoral promises and for structuring the administrative policies. At the same time, the bureaucracy which is permanent civil service in this country has a long experience about implementation of governmental and developmental programmes and, therefore, it is the responsibility of the bureaucracy to provide policy alternatives and to develop developmental programmes in consonance with the specific policy alternatives selected by the political hierarchy and by the political executive.

"It is very difficult to clearly indicate a dividing line where administrative policy formulation or alternatives end and the political executive's decision making role starts. In fact, decisions are often made through a discussion and a dialogue between the political executive and higher civil service. So to that extent it would be incorrect to think that whatever the politicians say or demand in terms of a stress on a particular kind of *Yojana* or in trying to say that there should be more poverty alleviation programmes or there should be greatest stress on employment, etc., is wrong or interference. We should not look at it as a dichotomy. However, at the same time in a developing country, where moral standards are not all that high, sometimes specific demands for helping or assisting people do come up. And sometimes when the upright officers deny these demands, they tend to suffer whereas others who are more pliable perhaps get some advantage in the short term. But, of course, if an officer is good and he is excellent in his work, has the confidence and the personality to put forward his point forcefully and to stick to his point, especially in relation to the requests for specific favours, in the long run this officer also does not do badly because political parties keep on changing, political fortunes fluctuate and sometimes, or the other, this straightforward person is also likely to be thrown up in the positions of significance. But at the same time, it is a real life sociological situation where there are pressures, some of these pressures are not of the right type and some people do buckle in, some withstand, some suffer, some gain and in this one should not always look at it as the political executive or the elected representatives are coming in way of the bureaucracy. Rather the effort should be to develop norms and institutions whereby the wrong kind of influences cannot harm the upright officers.

"In this regard, I would like to point out the practice in many states that finally the confidential roles of the senior servants are written by the minister. There have been cases where upright officers have to have the rough edge of the minister for obvious reasons. And when the officer makes a representation against such a remark, in many states or in some states, the body to which the representation goes is the Chief Minister, the Finance Minister and the Minister who had made the remarks and the Chief Secretary who is only a non-voting member in this committee. Furthermore, given the fact the political fortunes and majority are rather thin these days, it is sometimes unlikely that the Chief Minister would go against the remarks of his own colleagues. In such a case, the upright officer suffers. It may perhaps be desirable to look into this system. As far as possible the assessment of the officer should be limited to be made by the Chief Secretary or to the Chief Minister in consultation with the Secretary concerned and the Chief Secretary so that upright officers do not suffer at the hands of some Ministers who do not make the right demands. At the same time it is also necessary that in every department where matters are sensitive, committees of officers along-with one or two Ministers lay down policies so that no individual officer misuses his power and all observe basic norms or guidelines which have developed. In a political system, if politicians can be corrupt so are some officers who are not above all these things. This would, by and large, reduce the scope for discretion often misused. Discretion should only be available in areas where laying down of guidelines is very difficult. This is an area which has so far been neglected and needs to be paid more attention to''.

R.D. Kitson is of the opinion that in order to have a proper check on the day-to-day working of Railways, he would prefer to have real strong trade unions to get the department proper feedback about its functioning from time to time. He feels it would help Railways perform better. In Kitson's words:

''I feel we must have strong trade unions. There is no way we can survive unless there are positive trade unions. We must be criticised but it should be positive criticism. Out of a number of points made by the unions we can make out which are the ones which are legitimate and thus need to be undertaken and which are illogical and demanded just for the sake of it. It is necessary to have constant interaction with the unions. There is absolutely nothing wrong in it. But in the process what happens is that lot of power develops with the unions and I must admit that whosoever has said that power corrupts, it does happen like this. When you have powerful and strong trade union leaders over a long period of time, vested interests develop amongst them. That amounts to wrong and negative functioning and approach of the unions. That should not happen and to this extent we must be cautious because this leads to the situations which are counter-productive''.

With regard to political interference in the day-to-day administration, more so at lower levels, T.N. Chaturvedi holds the opinion that, ''An administrator must attempt to think about these problems alongwith doing this. I would like to say that saying of political interference in the administration by the functionaries is a kind of alibi also. From my own broad impressions and experiences, I can say that sixty to eighty per cent of what the administrator does is non-political, means not having any interference. On the remaining forty to twenty per cent there may be some pressure from some political leader or functionary. My point is that if we take care of the sixty to eighty per cent and decide it on merit of each case, by and large, the public image will be made. Once this image is made there is much less possibility of political interference or intervention and it would be much easier to do the remaining forty to twenty per cent also. Let us assume that there is political interference, if so, it tunnels down through the people at the top. At this stage the seniors must tell that this kind of interference is not proper. They must bring it to the attention and notice of the 'asking for' to not to press the administration for any wrongs.

''One also has to see how in a democratic process one looks at the political interference. Sometimes it may be a matter of caution for keeping administration on alert. I would call it as correct or popular interference or intervention. There is no use saying that because of political interference you cannot work. The administrators should go through each case and then firmly say 'no' if it is not within the rules. But it should not be 'no' for opposition leaders alonc and 'yes' for ruling party leaders. It would create further problems amounting to making administration political. We have to keep in view that the administration is a concern of the politicians because they have to deal with the people in general. So, there is a scope for this but I must say it should be constructive, positive, and corrective''.

Admitting that there is political interference in the administration, Kulandai Swamy feels that the administrators can do a lot to resist uncalled for interference. He has mentioned some important factors responsible for political interference. In his words, ''political leaders' interference is something that is normally complained about in any democracy, in any country. As a matter of fact, any politician who gets elected by the people will try to do something to please them. When it is to please the whole community there is nothing wrong; but when it happens to pleasing certain individuals, who might have been helpful to him, only then the problem arises. If you look at the people who were in position of ministers and holders of public offices immediately after independence, you will find they were all people who had held some positions as Chairman, District Boards, Municipal Corporations, or at least certainly as heads of autonomous bodies. They had held some responsibility and were held in high esteem by the people for their background, preparation, education, or family reputation, as the case may be. But election after election you will find more and more people from the lower stratum of society with lesser experience, lesser preparation get elected and are occupying positions of responsibility, as MLAs, and as Ministers. It is certainly a good trend: but they do not come with necessary knowledge and preparation for the responsibility they are to hold. This leads to more of interference in the administration because they consider their interests as the only interests. On the other end, the administrators do blame political leaders for their interference but at the same time the administrative functionaries are also inclined to take a very soft line. There are cases where the administrators have very happily and willingly colluded with the politicians often blaming them but at the same time looking for certain advantages, privileges and favour. I would not completely exonerate administrators and lay all the blame on the politicians alone''.

The police has a more visible role to play in the society. An action, wanted or unwanted, right or wrong, by the police leaves immediate impact and imprint on the concerned individuals. Everyone who is being rounded up by the police or who wants some police action to be taken in a given case would attempt to have the kind of pressure exercised upon the police by the political leaders, mostly of the local politicians, by the social group leaders, and even by the small groups of the localities. The major reason for this is again that police does not have a positive image of working speedily and judiciously. Vijay Karan says that ''India's police has, not an image, not even a non-image, but a positively bad image''. Such kind of image is responsible for having more pressures exercised on the police by all sections of the society. Another reason is the nature of police role itself.

In the opinion of Vijay Karan, ''It is doubtful if any other government agency performs such a strikingly negative role in society as the police. While the term 'maintenance of law and order' may sound positive, in actual terms, it means the practice of negativism in various forms: the regulating and stopping of people, not allowing the people to proceed to particular places, the fining of people, the searching and interrogating of people, the arresting and locking up of people, etc., go against the natural human urge of free will and generate not only unpopularity and even hostility, but also fear of the police. Such a kind of role leads to day-to-day interference of the political as well as social leaders' interference in telling the police to do this and to undo that''.

In the words of Arun Bhagat, ''The vested interests have become immensely powerful in our society. Take the case of electricity stealing or encroachment of a public place for opening a workshop or restaurant. When the parties or authorities concerned approach the police for support which we do provide, the persons who have done so consider it as police brutality and try to exercise all sort of pressures on the police. The permissiveness seems to have entered the society. I think a sense of greater responsibility is necessary in the society''.

Regarding dealing with the political leaders pressures, Vijay Karan said: ''It is true that a political leader might try to use the police for his own ends and would prefer the police to adopt extra-legal methods but if the police leaders are strong enough, I think they can resist these pressures''.

The training and orientation of political leaders would help them understand and appreciate the administrative procedures and practices in a better manner. H.S. Anand feels that it could lead to better understanding of the problems and positions of both sides. In Anand's words, ''I would fully agree that there is tremendous need for orientation of legislators. Not only this, there should be seminars and workshops where the senior administrators and legislators are brought together, are made to live together, and jointly participate in simulation and group exercises for appreciating each others' problems in a better way''.

B.B. Vohra has a different point of view regarding the training to be imparted to the political leaders. When asked to comment on this question, his reply was, ''This is a very tricky question to answer, very difficult question to answer. You see, all education is good *ipso facto*, training will help but how far it will help in the politicians giving up their basic interests is very doubtful. This is a real question. You can teach them anything you like theoretically but you should also find out the way of meeting their basic needs. This is a human question. It will be no use preaching the ideals and ideal form of behaviour without recognising the facts of life on the ground. So teaching is good but it shall have to be followed up by some way, for example holding the elections at the cost of the government or changing the whole pattern of elections''.

Kulandai Swamy holds firm opinion that political leaders need to be exposed to the problems and challenges being faced by the country and solutions to those in specifically conducted training programmes. He feels that it would also help them understand their obligations as well as the role, obligations, and constraints of administrators and also the administrative practices and procedures. He puts it thus: "The politicians may have the responsibility to the people but that is one thing. Their capacity to deliver the goods to the people is another. In such situations, it is always necessary that there is a mechanism or a facility by which these people can be exposed to the types of problems and kind of solutions and that too not one or two but many alternatives that are available and the manner in which the choice has to be made. As Vice-Chancellor Mudurai Kamraj University, I established Institute for Public Policy and Administration with the idea that we should hold periodic seminars to apprise the political leaders of the level of Panchayats and Municipal bodies about the problems regarding education, health, population, etc., being faced by their institutes and the solutions possible for the same. I thought that within a week or two they might get as much knowledge as they might otherwise gain after a year or two of experience in these institutions. In the modern world, there is hardly anything that one could do without necessary training and preparation. In a democracy, I think the quality of administration and the progress that a country can make would very much depend on political leadership. This has to be accepted, therefore, that whatever is done to improve the quality of political leadership is an investment that is worth making".

Commenting upon the role of universities in this regard, Kulandai Swamy, Vice-Chancellor for the last more than a decade said: "It is not just the problem of a minister at the centre or at the state. It is the problem of all MPs, MLAs, and of every small public office starting from the chairman of a gram panchayat. At each level, there is a kind of preparation, the kind of exposure that is needed. Perhaps educational institutions can take, as part of their extension activities, this responsibility and it can be tackled by every university in its own way. In such a context Indira Gandhi National Open University might play a wider role. But certain well defined institutions, specially for this purpose, are necessary. But more than anything else is the acceptance of the fact that these people need to go through this kind of training which is the first step. When that is conceded, everything else would follow".

V. Politicians Perceptions of Improving Administrative Responsiveness

Besides knowing from the selected political leaders and administrators their viewpoints regarding administration in India, its system, and its responsiveness, we have attempted to know from them points they have in mind which could improve the functioning of the administrative system and help making it more responsive.

Harkishan Singh Surjeet says that inefficiency in administration must be done away with and inefficient units, whether for production or in other sectors, should be streamlined. Responding to the question whether the privatisation could reduce the burden of the government thus leading to better administrative performance, Surjeet commented: "I don't think this is going to help because this will create fruther such institutions adding to the complexities. For example, the necessity is to improve those Public Sector Units which are in the red despite the best funds and technology available, rather than going in for privatisation. This is not going to solve the problem". He strongly feels that the system of working from both within and outside should be improved upon. Efficient persons and units must be encouraged as being trend-setters and eye openers for others.

Yashwant Sinha feels that the representative institutions at the lower levels should be strengthened and where these don't exist should be created. These would provide a good helping hand to the administrative units not only in undertaking the required developmental tasks but also in performing the regulatory functions in a proper way. He said, "I don't know whether privatisation is the solution to reduce the burden of work of administration and making it do well. He further added: "If I am, suppose, not member of the Parliament tomorrow that does not reduce my worth or my commitment to the people but will I get the same response from the administration which I get now? Probably, no! But I should". He is of the view that if he or anybody else belongs to a political party representing the people or even if he is from a non-governmental organisation, the administration must give hearing to him and the grievances and problems he brings forth must be sorted out if those are genuine.

Ram Jethmalani is of the view that those in the administration who have power to control the economic processes, those who come in contact with the industrialists, traders and businessmen and control their economic and fiscal activities do not feel burdened at all with the work-load. It is a self-imposed and self-acquired burden which they have. "These people have vested interests in continuing with the load because it provides them with an opportunity for corruption. The need is to divest them of their power. It is a burden to the honest few only. So it is true that divesting of power will go a long way to purify our administrative life and character of our administrators". He says that all are not corrupt, all are not crooked, there are some good persons also but the system does not permit honest people to hold power because from top to bottom a number of corrupt hands are easily available. It is essential to bring the corrupt ones to less important positions and the efficient and honest ones to significant positions.

Subramaniam Swamy feels voluntary organisations can play a substantial role in creating public opinion and suggesting to the administration what needs to be done. In his words:

"Voluntary organisations can create public opinion which will act as a pressure on the government. These organisations should go before the Parliamentary Committees, should hold press conferences, should go and meet the civil servants, give them suggestions and also threats of exposing them in public if the right is not done. Government functioning would respond to it but no government is going to voluntarily bring upon these organisations. These organisations should be social organisations for social common cause and not political organisations, like Rashtriya Swayam Sewak Sangh, which is a voluntary organisation in name but is used for political purposes. Voluntary organisations' positive working would facilitate administration do better"

He further says that there is need to streamline the basic structure of the bureaucracy. "The top heavy bureaucracy, this oppressive bureaucracy which we have needs to be streamlined and we must go for a competitive market economy. If we go for such a system people will get satisfaction from the government". Swamy is of the view that India must give up socialism and the citizens dependence on the government must be reduced. He said: "If the government is small and has fewer functions then the public will go less to it and may be the government could perform less functions better. This Russian model that we have adopted is the culprit behind the whole thing and must be done away with".

Advani besides suggesting the administration to be apolitical and the politicians not attempting to make it political holds the view that integrity, honesty and seriousness of purpose on the part of administrators can make administration do excellent job. The people's needs and wants would automatically be taken care of in the most prompt manner. He felt that the political leaders and administrators jointly frame the policy and a large number of our policies are the best but these are unable to give the desired results. He thinks the reason for this is faulty implementation. Advani said: "The political leadership is not expected to do much; it is the administrators at the lower level who have to do a lot and their performance to this effect is crucial because by that only the people's good can come about". He further said "If the administrators are conscious of it much could be done otherwise nothing concrete could be achieved in this direction".

Advani clarified the role of a policy framer and an implementor by quoting a small incident which was told to him. It goes thus: "When I was the chairman of the Delhi Metropolitan Council, we had the good fortune of having Mr. A.N. Jha as the Lt. Governor of Delhi and, of course, apart from his experience, he had his own flair of presenting things. He told me about the equation between a politician and an administrator. He recounted a very interesting anecdote. He said, a centipede once became afflicted with arthritis, and a centipede with so many legs and so many joints when it becomes afflicted with arthritis, you can imagine the kind of pain and agony it has to bear. So in that state of agony the centipede went to a wise owl and sought his counsel as to what to do? The owl shut his eyes for a moment and then opened and said, 'It is a simple thing, it can be easily done. You do one thing. You convert yourself into a crow so that instead of 100 feet you will have only two. So the pain will considerably get reduced'. Very happily, the centipede came home and told his children, 'I have got a solution for it' and children asked, 'what is the solution?' He said, 'the owl told me to convert myself into a crow. Children said, "how do you convert yourself into a crow?" The centipede said, 'I forgot to ask the owl; I have to go back once again'. And once again he went back to the owl and asked him, 'You did not tell me the full thing. How do I convert myself into a crow?' The owl remarked, 'I have dictated a policy. It is for you to implement it'."

When asked to comment whether bureaucracy can act as a good social and economic change agent through its responsiveness, Subramaniam Swamy stated, "I would say that bureaucracy is like a horse, the intelligent horse. If the rider is good, he will ride it far, otherwise it will go haywire". He feels that one of the ways to improve the responsiveness of the administration is to streamline the movement of files. Swamy observed: "Almost all kinds of petty files come to the Minister for signature. Is that necessary? It could be decided at the local level. Invariably, the delay is because every file is sent to the Ministry for clearance".

The bureaucracy must pick up courage of taking decision at its own level. Only the files of non-programmed nature issues may be put up to the Minister. The routine type issues should be sorted out at lower levels.

Swamy further said: "The concept of team work in the administrative units is not there. There is always a Master-Servant concept. It is a feudal concept. I think in the days when there is so much of unemployment in the country, where people cannot leave a job and find another, certain amount of slavish mentality comes in. The head of the unit gets the subordinates dance the way he likes because they do not want to be out of job or they do not want their career prospects harmed. The unity amounting to better work would be where there is team work, where the head inspires his subordinates to work. I would, therefore, like the government to be small and we should privatise most of the public sectors. The government, thus, will have fewer things to do and with less heavy, workload, it may be possible to have better quality work".

Yashwant Sinha is of the opinion that the administrators must talk to the public, listen to their grievances, and above all the level at which the public dealing is to take place must be clearly defined. He said: "Dealing with public should be taken as a very important aspect of administrators' functioning. He should not only be trained about how to deal with the public but he must be asked to set apart time for this purpose. You see, a politician, for instance, has to talk to people and listen to them. I can't hide myself now. But if I look at myself as an administrator and a politician, immediately the difference comes to my mind. As an officer, I was extremely reluctant to meet people at home but as a politician, I can't afford to do so, whatever time, day or night, whenever any visitor comes, I should meet him. I am not suggesting the same to an officer but he must set aside a time earmarked and notified that he would be available between such and such time for meeting the people, listening to their grievances. Once the citizens are able to meet him and he has listened to their grievances they will go back satisfied. Secondly, the level at which the public dealing will take place must be clearly defined. It will make people not to enter the Babus' office.

"Laxity has taken place in administration. One finds the Secretariats swamped by the people at the lowest levels because they don't get time with the high-ups in the administration. They go to the clerks. This is leading to not only breakdown in the functioning but also lot of corruption and malpractices are easily seen''.

Sinha further remarked about reestabilishing the practice of extensive touring and night-halts by the officers in the field, as used to be done during the British administration. He recollects that in early years of his service, ''the number of night halts made was a very important criterion for judging how well you are performing'' He is of the view that when an officer is on tour to a particular place under his jurisdiction and people come to know of it, they will approach him and whether willing or not he shall have to meet him.

Sinha feels that such an exercise would not only enable the people to get their grievances redressed but would provide a chance to the officer to obtain feedback about the performance of his office from the people. This would help a lot in bridging the gap between the citizens and the administration and would also help the administration establishing its credibility. He also said that the grievances of people must be immediately acknowledged and the action taken on the same conveyed to them.

VI. Administrators Perceptions of Improving Administrative Responsiveness

H.D. Shourie is of the view that the present-day functioning of the administration cannot improve substantially and probably no officer could do the same because of the laws and regulations existing in the country. Instead of solving, he feels, these are complicating the problems. Shourie opined ''The administrative responsiveness cannot be dependent on the individual head of any unit. Well, take the example of DESU. The employment in DESU is 30 thousand and similarly in some of the public sector enterprises like Railways, for instance. In the railways, I think there are about 18 to 20 lakhs of employees. You cannot expect the chairman of Railway Board to be able to get the things corrected.

''In the light of the fact that there is tremendous increase in the proliferation of the avenues of the development, proliferation of the functioning of the government, we have to now take stock of the totality and determine as to what changes in the laws may have to be done. For instance, nobody is at the moment aware what is the number of laws. There may be hundreds of thousands of laws operating in the country.

Now the situation is completely changed in comparison to the times when these laws were made. It is required that redundant laws and rules are done away with.

"Another major requirement is to have less of Government. As we are now thinking in terms of liberalisation and the removal of the controls on the industry, similarly, less of Government in every sphere of the activity, whether it is municipal committee, whether it is Tehsil, and so on is required. I don't think that under the given circumstances any administration could do well".

H.S. Anand feels that team work is a must for any unit of organisation to perform in a better manner. Alongwith this the head of the unit must have a reasonably long tenure so that he is in a position to make an effective use of his skills for the benefit of the unit, system, and its clientele. Anand opines that thorough training of the officials could facilitate their working but the training imparted must be made proper use of. In his words, "Proper team work and *esprit de corps*, is very vital for the deliverance of the objectives of administration. Sometimes officers are transferred very frequently. Just to quote a real life example, I worked to develop a particular corporation which was in the red and I managed to take the turnover from Rupees 4 crore to Rs 40 crore in two and a half years, just because I had security of tenure of about three years. Now on my leaving that corporation in a healthy state, because of having worked with my team to sustain it from an extremely bad position, I find that ever since I left it within a span of about two and a half years about 5 Managing Directors have changed. This means the average tenure of the particular MD has been about six months or even less.

"Now, this is another bane of the Indian politico-administrative system that quite often officers are transferred very frequently. Whenever there are elections in the states, each election or each change of Minister, mean substantial transfers which dislocate the work and this factor comes in the way of an *esprit de corps* being developed.

"Further, I would say that developing rapport and a team work with your line and staff also depends very substantially on the quality of inputs that you can put in. If your knowledge about the area that you are dealing with is reasonably good and you can show the lead, the line and staff is more willing to follow your directions. As you are well aware, you are an administrators' trainer, the Fulton Committee report in England had suggested that we must make out broad areas for specialisation. Which means that after spending a certain period as generalist in field operations when officers are actually serving as Sub-Divisional Magistrates or Additional District Magistrates or District Magistrates, they should be made to specialise in separate segments of the administration. For example, one segment could deal with social welfare related departments including education. Another group of departments could be related to Finance. A third group of departments could be related to agriculture and agricultural universities and associated departments, a fourth group of departments could relate to industrial development and the technical training and education. So we have to stream out the administration into very broad streams and after an officer having completed the initial period of generalist for about 10 to 12 years, he should be made to specialise in broad areas. For this purpose, I feel that they should be formally trained in India and abroad and personally I feel that they should undergo a structured course where there should be proper examinations. For example, if we send somebody to do M.Sc. in Development Administration with special reference to Industrial Development, let him do a two year course and let us see how he performs in the International college.

"We send officers for short specially designed courses. It is very difficult to assess how they perform whether they have spent most of their time shopping around and taking cosmos tours or whether they actually put in hard work. After receiving a properly structured training in which the officer is very carefully assessed and this assessment, like in the Army, should be considered as a very important ingredient in the future promotion prospects of the officers so that he is made to realise that his performance in this course is going to determine his future. These kinds of inputs can be made to make the officer a specialist in a given area of administration. This would enable the officer to have necessary depth of understanding, to provide necessary direction and to prove it be good leader for his team".

G. Ram Reddy, considers the head of the administrative organisation or sub-organisation as the key performer. It is his task to see that the job entrusted to his organisation is performed satisfactorily in the minimum amount of time and the clientele is happy about the same. Reddy feels that for this, "the supporting functionaries are to help the Chief Executive, collect information and bring it to the notice of the chief executive and should also advise him as and when required". Could there be any rules or guidelines for such kind of mechanism to be ensured? G. Ram Reddy firmly said: "No, you cannot lay down rules and much depends upon the personalities. There are bosses who work in co-operation with their colleagues, there are bosses who just don't trust their subordinates, there are bosses who treat the subordinates as their colleagues, there are those who treat subordinates as subordinates, they don't rely and they tend to centralise power in their hands. So it varies from person to person and only those who have a positive attitude towards administration and who believe in working in a co-operative manner can get the work done".

Regarding the role to be performed by voluntary organisations and non-governmental organisations, G. Ram Reddy thinks that, individually as well as collectively these organisations should work for the benefit of the system by getting above their vested interests, if any. The purpose and objectives of these organisations should be to help in making the administration responsive because this in itself would help them achieve their goals smoothly. Being Vice-Chancellor of different Universities for a long time and presently in the University Grants Commission as its Chairman, G. Ram Reddy feels that the role of the Universities, is to produce and disseminate knowledge in such a way which enables the learners to develop more sense of logic, understanding of the system, and to make them aware of their rights as well as duties towards fellow beings, the system, and the polity.

R.D. Kitson is thoroughly confident of the understanding and intelligent dealing of almost all the issues by the top Railway officials. They are all clear about what ought to be done and how it is to be done because they, in his words are "professional railwaymen". He says once the objectives are clear at the top there should not be any difficulty in giving direction down the line. But whether the directions are percolating down from the top professional echelon of Railway administration to the field in the proper way and also received accordingly, Kitson says that they are doing their best in providing opportunities to the lower staff to interact freely with the higher staff. They organise seminars, workshops, and orientation programmes which are attended by the senior and junior functionaries. He feels, "the effective communication has to be both ways". He said: "We can't sit idle, we have teams in hundreds of people always in the field inspecting, looking at works, checking records, and that is where the interaction comes. The contact is maintained. We have engineers who travel on trollies alongwith the line, they meet hundreds of thousands of gangmen. This is another way of interaction. I strongly believe that for better administration the head of the unit must have team work, better and effective communication not only with the colleagues but also with the public, and above all he must have a proper understanding of what he is to do and what his priorities should be".

T.N. Chaturvedi considers administrative responsiveness as the one having more of psychological dimensions in its fold which needs to be judged by more pedestrian parameters. He does not wish to plead for any wide range strategy for the same. What it needs is more of serious consideration and self-introspection by the administrators. It requires deep searching within on the part of administrative functionaries, political leaders, voluntary organisations, pressure groups and citizens to properly understand and appreciate the various facets of this multi-dimensional issue for arriving at a consensus for giving the society and the system a mechanism whereby all do their tasks and meet their obligations adequately. Besides this, Chaturvedi strongly holds the opinion that, "the rules and regulations in the total framework must have utmost amount of transparency, publicity, and nothing should be hidden so far as the routine things are concerned. For example, if the tenders are to be called for, it should be as open as anything. None should get the impression that the administration has nefarious designs of operation. Administrative discretions should be done away with. It would help in reducing the so called political pressures as well".

Looting at the issue of responsiveness of administration from another angle, Chaturvedi opines that the administration should not only be capacitated to deal with the existing conditions, situations and circumstances but should "be able to deal with the new circumstances, changing circumstances in the wake of socio-economic environmental changes. Otherwise, administrative responsiveness itself can become static, so it has to respond to the evolving needs, evolving standards, and evolving norms. The administration should not care for influentials of today but also of uninfluentials because may be the uninfluentials today become influentials tomorrow. For administration every one must be equal and same treatment should be accorded to all, which certainly should be positive and courteous".

For bringing the required changes in the administrative system which could go a long way in establishing its credibility, each administrator, Chaturvedi firmly said, should, "really have an idea of what is the mandate of a particular organisation in the system which has been handed over to him at a point of time for which he has responsibility as the bearer of authority today and may be the subject or object of it as a ordinary citizen tomorrow, work out the priorities and should make use of the discretion allowed to him within the limits and parameters of the authority, system's norms and system's values''.

Chaturvedi further adds that an administrator must pose questions to his own self: ''Do I look at the problem constructively without the initial negative bias and attitude? Though it could be or rather should be with the skeptical attitude, it is a must to have an attitude to ascertain by questioning whether a particular thing is possible or not. If possible, how to best deal with it and if not, then why and how could it be operated in the sense which does reflect my maximum administrative capabilities and acumen?; how do I identify the plans or special groups who are my clients and concerned with my way of administration from time to time?'' The former Home Secretary to Government of India and Comptroller and Auditor General of India, on the basis of his rich administrative experiences and immense knowledge of public administration as a discipline, feels that the reasons, like political interference, lack of infrastructural resources, etc., do not mean much and if the incumbent has the inclination to do something he can always find a number of ways to do that. Another related question Chaturvedi thinks, is how the administrators anticipate the problems of the future, developments in the future, emergent issues in times to come, and thus prepare themselves accordingly to cope with the quantum and needs of such futurist problems, issues, and developments. He said: ''The administration must have the sensitiveness to respond to the situation and must have the anticipatory antenna to identify issues''.

Lastly, Chaturvedi feels that the responsiveness must not go only with the responsibility and accountability, which to him are 'external checks', but it must have internal checks which mean an attitude of mind, how one looks at the problems of his clients considering as if it were his problems. One must have commitment to the professional standards of work. One must make him competent for doing the job he is expected to do, for developing self to cope with the new problems, if they arise. The commitment should not be to an individual politician, administrator, or political party but to the system. All the points put together will prove to be the beacon light for administrative responsiveness''.

Very briefly, but qualitatively, Kulandai Swamy has put forth certain much required aspects to be taken care of for bringing improvements in the deteriorating system for making it responsive. He said: ''The very first principle that must be accepted and implemented in this country is that if one is to administer medicine one should have a background of that subject, if one is to administer education, one should have a background of education. That a person is a pure administrator and he does not necessarily have to have any knowledge in depth of the subject proper is a fallacious philosophy that is widely prevalent in this country and to me it looks that it is the major weakness. Even if there is no political interference, as long as the administration suffers from this fatal inadequacy, it is not likely to be very successful".

Kulandai Swamy believes that in order to bring improvements in the system it is a must to adhere to the principle of professionalisation. Philosophically he said: "The deterioration takes place step by step. Any system is like a vertical pillar, if a vertical pillar is truly vertical then it is very easy to keep it in position but once it starts leaning, the more it leans the more difficult it becomes to hold it back to the original position. Professionalisation is likewise needed to not let the vertical pillar of administrative system leaning more and that again to the extent that it becomes impossible to put it back on the rails. Nowhere is the system where the real professionals work under the generalist administrators".

He feels that our administrators have enough security but are always under the grip of fear which does not permit them to work properly. He stated: "If people are to fear even small consequences for taking an independent decision there is no protection which could come to their rescue. There is a saying by Thiru Valluvar, one of our great poets, that for a person who suffers from fear there is hardly any fortress that could give him protection'. So a certain amount of moral courage is needed on the part of administrators also. I have always been maintaining that goodness does not consist of being harmless, goodness does not consist of just being helpful. Goodness really consists of fighting evil. Therefore, we should, as far as possible, mobilize support in favour of right kind of people in politics, whatever may be the party, so that they could in turn put administration on sound footings".

Referring seriously to the increasing load of work taken by the government on to itself and to the issue of decentralisation, the technologist in the Vice-Chancellor, Kulandai Swamy said: "As is being said from the very beginning of the establishment of democracy that state is the best which is least governed. So we should also ensure, as far as possible, that the kind of concentration of power that we see in our country today is drastically reduced. I have been a witness, as far as the last thirty years are concerned, to what has been a spectacle of publicly advocating decentralisation but practically augmenting centralisation.

This trend should not only be arrested, but completely reversed''.

Vijay Karan is of the view that the training which is imparted to the police functionaries is not up to the mark and it must be changed. He feels this could help police functionaries to perform better. In his opinion the coordinated manner in which the boss-subordinates need to function in a police station for making police administration more responsive should start at the training level. ''Whenever a policeman is recruited he goes through a training course at the level of Constable or Sub-Inspector or an IPS Officer. Normally the training is over a period of about one year. Unfortunately, during this training period hardly any lectures are delivered on police-community relations, on courteous behaviour with public, on responsiveness towards the public. No training has been given broadly to this effect. It is P.T., Parade, how to open fire, how to handle arms, etc., and law is taught but these basic inputs are lacking. What is required is also to tell them in details how they are to work with each other, how they are to deal with the public. They must be prepared to have pride in their uniform and in their organisation''.

Besides laying emphasis on training, Vijay Karan feels that the Indian police is functioning on the same old pattern as it used to during the British period. He said: ''Nobody tried to prepare a blueprint to bring about a total transformation of the police as it should function after independence. For this the blame lies basically with the police leaders because it should have been up to them to bring change. I don't blame political leaders for this because if the police leaders had wanted, then despite all political pressures on their otherwise working, they could have brought the change. I don't think political leaders could have opposed the change in the overall culture of the police.''

He further feels strongly about the need for having best possible Police-Community relationship as it would make the police more responsive and would help in improving its image and credibility among the people. He said, ''It is said that while a policeman is a policeman in uniform, a citizen is a policeman without uniform. So, that is why there has to be, I think, a sustained effort, over long period of time to build police-community relations. If we work with the people, I am sure we will then instil confidence in the people and if we work closely with them we will not do anything wrong, because if a policeman is working closely with a citizen, I don't think he will do anything wrong vis-a-vis the citizen. A policeman has a better image with a person whom he knows than a person whom he does not know. If you know a policemen at the social level also, I am sure he will be less high-handed towards you, he will be less corrupt towards you, whereas if you don't know him then he is more likely to be high-handed and demand money for whatever redressal you are seeking".

Regarding efficient and effective working of the police stations, Arun Bhagat is of the view that the work in these units should be subdivided by the head of each unit among his colleagues. He should not try to centralise all the things by himself. He must attempt through his efforts as well as those of his subordinates to get the maximum co-operation of the large section of public in his work jurisdiction. The response to the complainant should be positive and courteous. All these things combined, Bhagat feels, could help improve the system of police administration. He feels that the police is not getting due co-operation from the press. This is an important factor which stands in the way of police effors to establish its credibility among the public. In this regard Arun Bhagat's observation was: "Unfortunately, our media has not been playing a very positive role as they can and as they should. This is, of course, basically because they are concerned about their circulation. For that matter at times they exaggerate and blow out of proportion. I think their constructive role is necessary. This is what I always tell my friends in the media that it is alright to be critical but at the same time you must also bring out the good acts done by the police for the society, so that people can read that also rather than reading all bad things done by the police".

The views of some of top political leaders and administrators on the issues involved have been discussed. On the basis of their vast experiences the interviewees have talked about important facets of administrative responsiveness. The points emerging out of the views expressed by them have been analysed in the subsequent chapter.

References

1. Venkataraman, R. "The Role of Bureaucracy in Development Administration in India", speech delivered at the Lal Bahadur Shastri National Academy of Administration, Mussoorie, May 14, 1986.
2. Giriramaji, Pushpa, "A non-working government machinery", *The Times of India*, January 24, 1992.
3. Gandhi, Rajiv, "Responsive Administration", speeches made by Rajiv Gandhi in workshops of District Magistrates and Collectors, New Delhi, Government of India Press, p. 2.

4. *Ibid.*, p. 4.
5. *Ibid.*, p. 5.
6. Rao, P.V. Narasimha, ''Speech made at the National Institute of Financial Management, Faridabad'', January 15, 1992.

4

Analysis and Model Building

The perceptions and viewpoints of some of the top administrators and political leaders having varied and vast experiences to their credit are analysed and summed up in the succeeding text. These have been mentioned under four major headings: Indian administration and the state of responsiveness; Reasons for poor administrative responsiveness; the role of bureaucracy, political leaders, local elected institutions, voluntary organisations, and citizens have been analysed separately; Political leaders' and administrators' relationship as having impact on responsiveness of administration; and, tips for improvements, specifically for bureaucracy, political executives and leaders, local institutions, voluntary organisations, and citizens.

I. Indian Administration and State of Responsiveness

1. Administrative Responsiveness has Psychological Dimensions: The administration is not to the satisfaction of the majority of the people in India. Because of one reason or the other the various facets having place of prominence in making the system work for the ultimate benefit and welfare of the society are not performing their obligation in an integrated form. It has been noticed that the responsiveness on the part of administration is not just a sloganised statement which could be improved upon or ensured by pleading a single line strategy. It has psychological dimensions and has to be adjudged on the basis of the majority of persons' expectations and the performance of different rungs involved in it. It is not that easy to measure or quantify the quality of the responsiveness.

2. Responsiveness during British Rule: By and large, the response of the administration during the colonial rule towards the citizens was far better than what it is today. The common citizen was feeling more secure in the hands of the administration and did not have to face factors like corruption, favouritism, red-tapism, etc., to the extent he faces today. It is a fact that Britishers did not have many developmental functions but with regard to the running of day-to-day work of the government, the inhabitants did not have to encounter many problems. That is one of the reasons that people who have seen and experienced the British administration are left with no other alternative but to say that it was better than the present administration. Such a kind of thinking of even some of the citizens of an independent country that the alien rule was better does speak of the frustration and disappointments which the public is having now and reveals the performance of the administrative system and its functionaries.

3. *Solid Foundation of Indian Administrative System:* The present administration of india is based on the steel- frame of the Indian Civil Service and has inherited the same. Some of the present administrators and political leaders feel that the Indian administration has a solid foundation which it got as an inheritance from the British administration. Such a firm footing can help the present system to go ahead for bringing more and more positive changes in its working in accordance with the new thrust, orientation, and commitment of the polity and system to the citizens of the country.

4. *Expectations for Change in Administration after Independence:* After the 15th day of August 1947 the citizens of independent India did expect a big change to come in the administrative working and the administrators' attitude. Overnight people had got the feeling that it is their government now which would be working for no other purpose but exclusively for the welfare of the society. For that matter any person who would find a change, a major change, in the polity would crave for such new things to come to the fore. Though people had some appreciation for the regulatory administration of the British, yet now they wanted to have the administration work on regulatory as well as developmental tasks in a more fruitful manner to the satisfaction of the people.

5. *Responsiveness is Poor:* The present state of working of the administration is throroughly bad and dismaying. It seems that the administrative functionaries have no care and concern for the common man. The important components of the government, that is, political

and permanent executive, are not working in a cohesive manner as a result of which the expectations of the people from their own government are far from being fulfilled. The citizens have developed a mistrust for administration. The common citizen feels that unless he has money or other influential factors with him, his right, genuine and even deserving work would not be done. The administration has not a good or positive but a poor, bad and negative image in the minds of the public. The quality and degree of response of the administration to the genuine and just needs, demands and wants of the citizens is poor and weak.

6. *Administration is Indifferent to the People:* A democratic political system, has to have an administration which carries out the policies enacted by the representatives of the people executed in a speedy and effective manner whereby the benefits go to the maximum of the concerned. Unfortunately, the Indian administration through its officials has lost the human touch. It is taking everything as a case and a file which has no entity and the man dealing with the file in the administration is more lifeless than the file itself. None is ready to adopt the required attitude towards the masses. The kind of concern, kind of impression or imprint to be left on the minds of the public, is not being taken care of at all by the administration.

7. *Responsiveness to be in Conformity with the Expectations:* As stated earlier, the administrative responsiveness has psychological dimensions and is not merely a sloganised statement. The responsiveness on the part of the administration could always be ascertained on the basis of the kind and level of expectations of the people. Viewing it from this angle, one finds that the Indian administration is not performing as per the expectations of the people. The administrators feel that the expectations of people have increased manifold. Why should it not be so? Comparing with the other sections of the society, the administrators are better placed than others and the system has given them the privileges and status. Then how come the expectations of others are not termed as just. Moreover the expectations of the citizens are from the polity, from the system and the administration is only a service-oriented agency and not the ultimate authority. Whatever the case may be, the response of the administration to the expectations of the citizens is much short of being satisfactory.

II. Reasons for Poor Administrative Responsiveness

The political leaders and administrators have tabled forth a number of factors as responsible for poor administrative responsiveness. These are mentioned below under five different sub-heads.

A. Bureaucracy

The permanent executive has the major role to play in implementing the policies for various developmental tasks and also for functions with regard to regulation of the day-to-day administration. Stated below are some of the points which reveal the part played by the bureaucracy in adding to the lack of responsiveness of the administration:

1. *Cautious and Callous:* The administration is too much cautious. The bureaucratic functionaries do not wish at all to go out of the rules and regulations. On the face of it, there does not seem to be anything wrong in functioning as per the prescribed rules but the bureaucracy at the same time should never forget that it is dealing with living beings and not dead woods. For the fear of being punished, in case, something wrong is done, the bureaucracy tends to be extra-cautious and does not like to own responsibility for anything. This over-cautious approach coupled with the callousness on the part of the functionaries is getting the system a very bad name and image. Furthermfore, one's callousness is at the cost of a number of citizens of the country. Nobody seems to understand the difficulties and the problems caused to others by the callous approach of those who have the responsibility of working for the welfare of the society.

2. *Inefficient:* Any person who wants to get even the smallest and simplest issue sorted out by the bureaucracy, that too within the vast and fair orbit of rules and procedures, undergoes a lot of harassment because of inefficiency of the system. There is hardly any case which gets decided in time on merits. People have to go from pillar to post and still what they face is not success. Most of the people have stopped visiting the offices because of the fact that nothing is to come out of it. But to what an extent such an inefficient work mechanism could go? How long the people shall have to be oppressed by the administration?

3. *Vested Interests:* It is a fact that the prime thing for any human being is his self-interest. But should we be so self-centred that we tend to forget what basically are we supposed to do? The bureaucratic machinery has developed vested interests. The administration is becoming more and more political and corrupt. For protecting their own interests, the officials keep on putting the citizens to a great loss and, by and large, the responsiveness of the system of administration now appears to be talk of yester years alone and without the hope for its revival.

4. *Lack of Clarity of Objectives and Goals:* Most of the implementors at the lower echelons of administration do not have absolute clarity of objectives and goals. In order to attain the targets which are placed before them by the high-ups they do all sort of proper or improper things for showing the targets as attained. Any person without being clear as to what he is to do claiming that he has completed the targets in itself reveals what kind of work must have been done. The functionaries at the district level and below feel strongly that the policy statements are not self-explanatory, clear, and are contradictory and conflicting and they don't easily get the required clarifications from higher levels. Unless the implementors are clear of what and how a thing is to be done, to expect an efficient and appropriate functioning from them would be chasing a wild goose. Lack of clarity of policy, its goals and objectives is one of the important reasons for the lack of responsiveness of the administration.

5. *High Headedness:* The government functionaries have no respect for the dignity of their clients, that is, the citizens. The officials consider themselves to be too superior than the persons approaching them and feel that anything which they are doing, virtually as a part of their duty, is in the shape of favours being done to the public. Such high and strong headedness and the kind of superiority complex in their thinking is not getting the people what is due to them. Though in a number of states, the government has started '*Mukt Dwar*', '*Weekly Darbars*', where the people's grievances are heard, still a commoner can not expect to be given a chance to be heard by the concerned official with patience. The Indian civil servants have forgotten that they are to serve the society.

6. *Personality Split:* Every person is first a citizen and then anything else. A teacher, a doctor, an advocate is first a citizen and then a teacher, a doctor, or an advocate. Same is true of an administrative

official also. But, unfortunately, the administrators (that holds true of others also) are not ready to accept the hard fact that being first only citizens, it is the present system which has given them some responsibility and authority and it is a gift which God has given them. This split in the personality of the functionaries does not make them think what the magnitude of any person's problem could be for him. Such thinking on the part of the administrators does not let the system function for the welfare and benefit of the sizeable number of citizens.

7. *Long Hierarchies:* The file in the administration has to cover innumerable paces. One simple case has to pass through so many channels and this results in enormous delays. Why cases of similar nature are not decided at the initiated level only, why it has to be dealt with again and again by a number of functionaries. The huge administrative organisations have long and seemingly unending hierarchies. Even if the decision ultimately is to be made in favour of the claimant, yet the procedure involved takes so much of time that the citizen gets disheartened, not only this, it breeds corruption as well and all these factors add to the already miserable state of functioning of the system.

8. *Rules and Regulations:* The maintenance of office records, lack of proper training, increasing number of policies and rules coupled with earlier rules framed by the Britishers in a majority of cases are responsible for the administration not functioning in the required way. The administrative leaders must logically present to the government that the rules and regulations which are obsolete and serve no purpose in the wake of developmental policies and overall socio-economic changes in the society on the basis of rules should be done away with. The knowledge of the performers of the new rules is far short of being satisfactory. Thus the delay and wrong decisions causing loss to the public.

9. *Quantum of Work:* The workload of the administrators, because of new policies, law and order disturbances, terrorist activities, unrest, etc., has increased substantially. Of course, the number of agencies and functionaries has also gone up but the proliferation of the government in more and more areas is an important factor in the increase of the quantum of work to be performed. Shortage of manpower is always considered a big problem and threat to the speedy working of the administration.

10. Use of Discretion: The administrative functionaries, when they are interested in doing some work, may be because of the political pressure, social pressure, personal whims, are always able to find a way out and use their discretion. Use of discretion is rather good but the way it is used for some special cases reflects the bias in the thinking and working of the administration and spoils its overall impact and image. Using discretion in one case and deciding another case of the same type differently makes people feel that the administration is not for the common citizenry but for the influential citizenry. These factors create a gap between the administration and the citizens.

11. Motivation: It is an admitted fact that the human beings are the most important resource of the organisations and the motivated functionaries contribute a lot towards the accomplishment of the objectives and goals. The functionaries in Indian administration find more factors which demotivate them instead of motivating them. A demotivated official would never be in a position to do his best rather at times it won't be wrong to expect an intentional error being committed because of his frustration and dissatisfaction with the system. When the honest officials are to be side-tracked and the dishonest are to be placed on positions of importance, one could not expect rightful functioning. The officials in the system are not motivated at all.

12. Inspiration: The seniors in any organisation are the biggest and most important source of inspiration for their subordinates. In administrative organisations one seldom finds superiors who think it proper, because of their ego, strong headedness, lack of clarity, etc., to even talk to the subordinates. To think of any senior inspiring the juniors is probably not a tradition in the Indian system of administration. In turn, what percolates down is the wrong practices and corrupt means adopted by the seniors which give a hint to the juniors also to work accordingly.

13. Training: The culture of training does not hold ground in India so far. Officials do not feel that they could be trained. Once an individual joins a government organisation, he feels that he is the best and the most knowledgeable person in the total system and is equipped to perform each and every thing. Besides, the training endeavours being made by different institutions and organisations are not up to the mark whereby some concrete results could be witnessed. Because of the new developments, new policies, rise in expectations, it becomes more important to lay substantive emphasis on the training but here it is the other way round. The resultant is that the functionaries are unable to perform what is expected of them.

14. Improper Protection: It is often said by the lower levels of administrators that there is tremendous amount of pressures from political leaders and they are unable to work judiciously because of this. They feel that if they don't work according to the dictates of politicians they have to face the music. Their seniors at the Directorate and Secretariat levels are not ready to protect them and so they do not feel like taking cudgels with the politicians. Such indifferent attitude of the seniors towards their juniors (not only this, at a number of times the political pressures are tunnelled through the top administrators) conveys the message to the lower staff to function in a wrong and subdued manner.

15. Supervision: Proper monitoring, and evaluation is a must for ascertaining the rightful functioning of the performers. The mechanism in existence in the administration for this purpose is not up to the mark. Besides, the top leadership in different organisations and sub-organisations is not providing appropriate lead and supervision to the functionaries. Lack of supervision and timely feedback to the subordinates is responsible to a considerable level for not ensuring effective functioning of officials at different lower rungs. At times the so called top leadership in the administrative units is not having clarity of the things by itself, so it is not possible to expect adequate supervision from them. All this brings laxity in the administration causing delays, corruption, and nepotism.

16. Unethical: The administrators ought to possess a code of ethics, moral standards and values. The present scenario reveals a picture whereby, to a major degree, the ethics has vanished away from the functional styles of the administrators. The administration is unethical, inhuman, and immoral. The degradation in values is responsible for the poor administrative responsiveness. The material urges are predominating the functionaries as a result of which a majority of them have become morally and financially corrupt. It has resulted in not clearing any file without the element of gratification. The citizens have to pay for any thing they want to get through. Middlemen are found everywhere and these touts help the functionaries and themselves at the cost of not the citizenry alone but also the system as such.

The administrators and political leaders interviewed for the purpose of this work have pointed out the above said factors as responsible for the lack of responsiveness and for which the onus lies on the administration.

B. Political Leaders

The permanent executive is not the only one who has a role to play in ensuring administrative responsiveness. The political executives and leaders also have an important part to play in this. On the basis of the interviews, the counts on which political leaders are responsible for adding to the lack of responsiveness of the administration are analysed below :

1. Policy Statements: The major task of the political executive is to formulate the policies and the permanent executive is to execute the same. Both of these cannot be divorced from each other as the permanent executive has also a role to play in policy formulation and the political executive in policy implementation. But broadly the major functions are formulation by political executive and implementation by the administration, of course, each having some role in both. The policies framed are not clearly worded, have lots of legal terminologies, contradictions, and are not self-explanatory. Such ambiguous policy statements and pronouncements are not easily understood by implementors. Lack of clarity stands in the way of doing full justice to the same in an effective manner. As a result of this the citizens do not get their due in appropriate time.

2. Politicians' Attitude: Compared to the period in 1950s and early 1960s, there is a lot of change in the attitude and thinking of the politicians. They have started taking the nation, its rules, its values, etc., for a ride. The respect and regard which they used to have for the administrators and also appreciation for their constraints are no more being witnessed now. The political leaders want to make headway at the cost of each and every thing. The administrators are considered simple tools to toe the lines of the political leaders. The handle of transfers is often being misused. All these actions of the politicians have made the administrators more and more defensive and they do not want to be in conflict with the political leaders at the cost of their service career and advancement. Such conflict between the two is proving to be bad for the system and the society.

3. *Uncalled for Pressures:* The political leaders have become more and more demanding. For every thing they consider it their basic right to interfere and intervene in the functioning of the administration. The political leaders want to get the interests of their selected favourites protected. There is no contest for the point that the political leaders are responsive and responsible to the people. But are they bothered about the common lot of the citizens? Certainly not. They are concerned with only those who could get them something. As the common public find the administration to be the task of bureaucracy, so it blames the bureaucracy more when it is found that so and so leader could get something undue to such and such from the administration. The fact of the matter is that a person who does not have linkages cannot even meet a political leader. Despite the best efforts of the authors of this book, three former top political executives and leaders of the country could not be contacted for an interview for ascertaining their views on this aspect. The crux of the matter is that the political leadrs want to get wrong things done by the administration by pressurising them in all possible unjust manners.

4. *Norms and Standards:* The ethics, the values, the norms, the moral standards which the political leaders should follow, seem to have withdrawn from their functional dictionary. Innumerable instances could be quoted where for achieving their own petty ends, the governmental functioning has been kept at stake. Lack of required political functionaries' norms and standards are responsible for demoralising, spoiling, and corrupting the administration.

5. *Populist Policies:* The political executive for the sake of making inroads into the vote banks attempts to impress them by announcing that such and such policies are made which would be able to give abundant benefits to the society. Most of such populist announcements are never converted into policies at all, some of those on which the policies are made do not cover as many sections of the society as announced, or the benefits earlier announced are not provided for in the policies in the same quantum. All these populist actions on the part of the political executive make the administration pay a very heavy price and contributes in creating a bad image of the administrative agencies among the masses. The citizens go by what political announcements are made and immediately start circling around the government offices for getting the benefits as per the announcements. They are not aware whether the

policies have actually been made or not and if so what is it about and to whom and to what extent the benefits are to be accorded. When the administration most genuinely feels helpless in getting them the benefits in the absence of the policy or not on the lines which were announced, the people develop the feeling that the administration is inefficient and unwilling to help the people. This widens the gap between the citizens and the administration without either party being at fault.

C. Local Elected Institutions

The popularly elected institutions also have a role to play in making the administration not responsive. The political executive, the administrative system, and the local institutions' leadership are all responsible for these institutions at the local level not performing what is expected of them.

1. Weak Political Position: The local institutions, may it be Municipal Corporation, Municipal Committee, Town and Area Committee, Cantonment Board or Notified Area Committee at the city or town level or Gram Panchayat at the village level, Panchayat Samiti at the block level, and Zila Parishad at the district level have not only the capacity to keep a check on the concerned government level but can also make the administration undertake the tasks in the order of the local priorities and needs. But, unfortunately the political position and status of these local institutions are very weak. At a large number of places these are either superseded, suspended, or dissolved. At some places where they are in existence, the local bodies are unable to do what is expected of them. As said earlier, the administrative system is also responsible for the weak position of these bodies because the administration does not want any competing agency in its work jurisdiction. The result is that neither there is any check which could have been there by these bodies on the administration because of the public support with these bodies, nor the administration is able to get assistance from these bodies in the form of popularising itself among the masses and seeking co-operation of the people.

2. Poor Leadership: The leaders of the local bodies are the ones who represent the local public. These local leaders neither possess the requisite leadership qualities nor do have the talent to put their point of view strongly before the administration. At times it is observed that the local leaders for protecting their own interests fall in the lap of the administration and leave themselves absolutely at the disposal of the administration. In case the administration uses them or does not take them into confidence for going ahead, both ways the functioning of the administration, revealing its concern for or response to the public gets affected.

3. *Weak Financial Position:* The local bodies are financially very weak. As a result these bodies have to look towards the state and the district administration for financial assistance. This situation does not enable the local bodies to do anything constructive whereby it could provide a helping hand to the administration in building its credibility and responsiveness. Overall, it could be said that the local bodies could be made an effective tool for the same and the lack of it affects the responsiveness.

D. Voluntary Organisations and NGOs

The voluntary organisations and a number of non-governmental organisations which have come up over the years appear to be more busy in prospering themselves than to relieve the administration of its burden in some cases and trying to mobilise public cooperation for the administration thus facilitating its operations. Even in a number of such organisations one finds the government officials occupying a place of prominence. In fact, a parallel bureaucratic structure is witnessed in the majority of these organisations which by its own self is not as per the basic features of such organisations. Dependence on the government for finance, for getting areas earmarked for its operations, for lands and subsidies, these organisations are not able to do what they could have done by providing a check on the functioning of the administration on one end and by getting the administration due co-operation on the other. These acts or performance of such type does affect the responsiveness of the administration or one could term it as a reason for the lack of responsiveness of the administration.

E. Citizens

Normally, the citizens can be dividied into three different categories. One is of those who belong to the business community and possess a good amount of wealth . These people on the basis of their affluence can influence the administrative functionaries for getting their work done. These people do have good contacts with the political leaders as well. The number of persons belonging to this category is not large. The second category is of those who are in the service class or in middle class business. These people do have some contacts, on the basis of their position in the society, with the administration and also with politicians in a few cases. The professionals of the middle rung also fall in this category. The third category is of those who neither have money, nor position in the society because of their service, profession, or business but are the deprived lot. These are the common men and are in a majority in this country. In fact, they are much more in number than the combination of the first two types. The question which arises is whether the citizens have some role to play in making administration responsive and which of their acts and deeds stand in the way of the administration not being responsive. The citizens are held responsible to some extent for the administration not being responsive on the following counts:

1. *High Expectations:* It is said that with the change in the political system after independence, with more thrust on developmental activities, and with emphasis of the government on equality and social welfare, etc., coupled with more and more burden having been taken by the government onto itself, the expectations of the citizens have gone up considerably. People want to get the maximum from the administration without the least delay and do not want to be put to any kind of inconvenience. Unfortunately, the rights of the citizens and whatever is due to them is always being remembered by the citizens and at times they are more demanding even unjustifiably. When their so called unjust demands are not complied with or there is even minor delay in compliance of their just wants and needs, the citizens go all out to accuse the administration. Rarely the citizens attempt to co-operate with the administration with the same enthusiasm with which they want to get their work done by the administration.

2. *Self-Interests:* Citizens are very possessive about all the rights to be conferred upon them and want to get all the benefits in one form or the other. Seldom one finds the citizens giving attention to their obligations and duties also. The administration and citizens have to go alongwith each other and none of the two should try to outsmart the other for personal ends. For the sake of protecting their self-interests citizens do

not mind bribing the functionaries for getting their cases sorted out without delay. Innumerable instances of such forced bribing of the functionaries by the citizens are there. One just can not blame the administrative functionaries alone. Lack of co-operation from citizens, insistence on the part of citizens for getting their right or wrong, just or unjust issues sorted out are to some extent responsible for the administration not becoming as responsive as required.

3. *Lack of Awareness:* It is a fact that till date the majority of Indian citizens are not educated enough to understand the mechanism of administrative functioning, its rules, procedures, and above all the constraints of administrativc officials. Even educated people and professionals do not have enough awareness of these things. Without having a proper knowledge of what a thing is about and how it is to be dealt with, the citizens want the administration to do their work immediately. The problems, constraints, and difficulties of the officials are not appreciated by ther citizens. The result is the disappointment which the citizens go through when their work is not done and this disappointment ultimately widens the gap between the citizens and the administration. Even in a family, the mother or the father would not respond to the unjust demands and wants of the children. But nowhere it is alleged that the parents are not responsive to the children. It is a misfortune that the citizens, by and large, do not consider the government and the administration as their own or to which they belong.

In the five sub-sections, we have analysed the role of bureaucracy, political leaders, local elected bodies, voluntary organisations, and citizens in not making the administration responsive. In other words, the reason for the lack of administrative responsiveness, as put forth by the distinguished interviewees have been analysed.

III. Political Leaders-Administrators Relationship

Another dimension of prime importance in making or standing in the way of responsiveness of the administration is the relationship between the political leaders and the administrators. An analysis of the perceptions of our sample of work is made in the following five sub-points:

1. *Politics and Administration cannot be Separated:* As discussed

earlier, the roles performed by both the political leaders and the bureaucrats in making and executing the policies are such that a line of division between the two cannot be drawn. Both have to work with each other for a better and meaningful performance of their obligations. Both the partners are most important not only in their distinct areas but also for each other. For example, while the political executive has the ultimate authority, the permanent executive has all the authority to give true shape to whatever the political authority wants. If political leadership is responsible to the people, the bureaucracy is responsible to the system. It would, therefore, be wrong on the part of either the politician or the administrator to think that one could be viewed in isolation from the other.

2. *Political Leaders are more Responsible to the Citizens:* A number of administrators-- more so at the district level-- often feel that political pressure and interference in their day-to-day working is enormous. A majority of the administrators contacted by us for eliciting their views, have stated that political leaders have to be more responsible to the citizens for two reasons. Firstly, they have to fulfil the promises they have made at the time of the elections, and secondly, they and their parties have to face the citizens again after five years for seeking their co-operation and support in elections. So if the political leaders show interest in administration, it should not be termed as interference but rather the administrators should feel happy by working in close co-operation and cohesion with political leaders.

3. *Political Pressure in Limited Cases:* Though political pressure on the administration is generally talked about, yet none has been able, in the administration at the lower levels, to quantify the pressures. On top of it, the top administrators feel that in around sixty to eighty per cent of the administrative tasks there is no pressure at all. It could be there in around twenty to forty per cent of the cases. Taking averages out of these figures, one could make out that in seventy per cent of the cases the administration has a free hand to operate and in thirty per cent there may be some pressure. If the work performed by the bureaucracy in the seventy cases out of every one hundred is judicious, right and just, a great possibility could be that the amount and level of the thirty per cent pressurised cases also get reduced substantially. The functionaries under the garb of political pressure on them in some limited cases have made it a ground to do a number of wrongs in other cases as well.

Probably, they feel that if two cases they are deciding on the recommendation of a politician then six of those kinds they should do on their own as per their interest and they conveniently pass the buck of all this on to the politicians as their pressure on the administration.

4. *Nothing Wrong in Political Check and Pressure:* It has been observed, on the basis of views garnered from different prominent personalities, in politics and administration, that in a democratic polity if there is political pressure or check on the administration by the political leaders, then there is nothing wrong in it. Firstly, because the ultimate responsibility of steering the nation or the state towards betterment is that of the political leadership which has the ultimate authority. Secondly, the commitment of the politicians to the electorate makes them ensure sound administration for the benefit of the masses at large. The corrective pressure or check on administration could rather help in bringing up the responsiveness of the administration in a more concrete and positive manner.

5. *Officials Succumb to Political Pressure*: As a result of poor institutionalisation of their services, their own vested interests, their own corrupt practices and means, the officials try to please the political leaders by telling them different ways whereby they could make good fortunes through illegal means. To say that the officials are responsible to some extent for corrupting the political leaders won't be an exaggerated observation. In order to make a headway for themselves undeservingly the officials do not resist pressures from the politicians but rather easily succumb to the same.

The dealings, fair or under the table between the political leaders and administrators at the behest of one or the other, certainly have a good amount of positive or negative effect on the responsiveness of the administration. Instead of attempting to find faults with each other, the best for the system is that both must evolve a mechanism which could contribute effectively to the building up of a responsiveness administration.

IV. Tips for Improvement

After ascertaining the views and perceptions of different distinguished personalities regarding the state of the administration in India, the quality of administrative responsiveness and the reasons for poor responsiveness, we had asked them to suggest ways for improvements by which the administration could become more responsible and responsive to the people and the system. The views collected have been analysed in the following text under five sub-categories.

A. Bureaucracy

The bureaucracy is the main actor in administering the affairs. The emphasis thus is more on improvements to be ushered in the administrative structure in comparison to the others. The following suggestions have been made in this respect.

1. *Streamlining the Structure:* It has been suggested that for undertaking the work by the bureaucracy in the best possible manner it is necessary to first streamline the structure of the bureaucracy and make sure what is required and at what place. There is no need to have more and more of positions and creating work for these. We first create an office or a position and then think of the work to be allotted for that. It should rather be the other way round. The result has been that the positions and agencies have increased substantially and there is overlapping in a number of cases. Such overlapping and references made by one agency to the other often leads to functional delays. There is dire need to streamline the basic structure of bureaucracy in this country.

2. *Organisational Development:* The quantity and quality of the work to be undertaken by different agencies has increased. Efforts for ushering in development in the administrative organisations are rarely seen. We are not passing through static phases. Because of the developments taking place in and around the existing organisational environment, the working of the organisations of the administrative agencies is being affected. The leaders of the administrative units must endeavour to develop their organisations to cope with the quantum of tasks as well as with the rapidly changing environment around the units.

3. *Team Work:* No person in any organisation is competent and capable enough to take all the work on to himself. Team spirit has to be developed in the administrative units whereby all the people involved in accomplishing a task are taken into confidence and take pride in working for that organisation. *Esprit de corps*, or team spirit, is rarely

seen in our administrative organisations. This affects the output of the administration both in quality as well as in quantity. Team work must be emphasised upon so that all feel concerned in undertaking the work collectively.

4. *Clarity of Objectives and Goals:* It is unfortunate that even the so called heads of the administrative units at the district level and below are not clear about a good number of policies and the objectives and goals thereof. Such lack of clarity on their part does not permit them to plan out their work schedule in a detailed and specific way. It amounts to delays and breeds corruption. There must be absolute clarity of the goals, policics, and what is to be done.

5. *Leadership:* The leaders of the administrative sub-units or sub-organisations have an inflated ego. They do not consider anybody else as competent enough. Lack of clarity of objectives, false ego, and an autocratic style of functioning on the part of these leaders are some of the important reasons which do not allow the agencies to perform the way these are required to. Following the leaders, the followers in the subordinates also start behaving in an obstinate manner with the common public. The need is for the leaders to have a sound leadership style keeping the situation and circumstances in view. The actions of the leaders can take their units to commendable heights.

6. *Self-Introspection:* Any administrator thinking that all others around, including the politicians, the citizens, the seniors and the juniors are incompetent, dullard, corrupt, lethargic, more demanding, etc., is probably doing the biggest injustice to them. Such a person thinks himself to be the only wise and perfect administrator. Well, if someone has such qualities it is good for the system but one should also have in mind that if all feel so at their respective ends then where the ills are. Better it would be that an administrator makes self-introspection and a deep searching of himself by putting questions to oneself: What am I doing?; Is it fair?; Am I clear how, when and why it is to be done?, etc. Such self-introspection can make the functionary clear about his own doings and whenever he is wrong he could improve upon that. If all start thinking like this most of the wrong things in the system of administration would come to an end.

7. *Innovativeness:* Change is the law of nature. The situations

prevailing in the period immediately following independence were not the same in the late 60s and 70s and similarly what the situations were in the 1970s are not what they are today. Likewise, what would be in the beginning of the 21st century would be entirely different from what it is today. The procedure of work at present should not be what it used to be earlier. The administration ought to be innovative for coping with the developments and changes. The administration must prepare itself to deal with the emerging issues. It would be possible if the administrative officials have not only a sound vision to foresee things and anticipate problems to prepare in advance for meeting with the same but also should devise ways to undertake the present work at hand with better and innovative skills and ways. It would reduce the hazards in the administration and facilitate its way to be more responsive to the needs and wants of the people.

8. *Delegation:* Authority should not be concentrated in the hands of the top levels alone. The authority to deal with the cases must be delegated to the concerned levels where the cases are to be dealt with. This would not only give a feeling of involvement and concern to the lower levels but would also help in sorting out the issues at the appropriate levels without referring each and every case to the high-ups which causes delays and harassment to the applicants/complainants. Besides, it would provide a chance to the functionaries to develop themselves and work with more responsibility. Furthermore, it would reduce the burden of routine work being performed by the top leaders who could best utilize their time for other important issues.

9. *Efficiency and Effectiveness:* The administration should not only be efficient but also effective. There is no point in deciding a case unless its benefits reach the concerned quarter. Efficiency cannot be there unless the functionaries are given authority, team spirit is inculcated in them, proper leadership is provided, timely feedback is there, efforts are made to effectively monitor and supervise their activities, and they are made to take actions in a manner whereby the decisions taken by them are made effective through quick actions.

10. *Communication:* Normally, communication in the administration moves from the top to the bottom. This is not a sound system or mechanism of communication. It should be ensured that it is both ways. The top level of the administration should encourage the functionaries

from below to interact with them. This would not only make things clearer to the lower echelons helping them to speedily perform their duties but would also instil confidence in them which would, in the long run, facilitate the administrative system to perform better. Primarily the onus for encouraging and welcoming upward communication lies with the top but once it is there it becomes the duty of the bottom also to come out of their shells to interact firmly and confidently with the top. More than fifty per cent of the citizens problems could be sorted out promptly through a proper communication between different channels in the administration.

11. Interaction with the Public: Right from the top to the bottom, the functionaries need to be prepared to the effect that they are to serve and not boss over the citizens. They are not their masters at all. Courtesy, disseminating proper information, of course, without leaking out the secrets, telling them the procedures, helping them in a proper way, etc., are some of the things which could make administration win over the confidence of the public. The senior officers must make extensive touring of their areas, meeting people, meeting functionaries, and trying to act as a bridge between the public and local functionaries at positions at far away places by listening to the citizens and the functionaries in the presence of each other and building confidence of both. It would help the administration improve upon its otherwise negative image to move over to a positive one.

12. Transparency in Working: The administrators should not act in a very secretive manner. Even if an action is just, it gets the impression to all concerned that there is something suspicious in it. There should be transparency in the working. It would not do as much harm as the lack of it is doing. Being more secretive and acting in a hidden fashion is rather building a wall of suspicion between the citizens and the administration.

13. Motivation: Government functionaries are the most demotivated lot. A number of reasons are there for this. More than the financial incentives, the non-financial incentives could motivate the functionaries. For example, the honest few in the set-up are not given key positions. The dishonest are rewarded through good postings at best stations. There is no appreciation of the good work done. Instead of appreciating the hard worker, the sycophants are found closer to the top administrative heads. These points play a substantive role in demotivating the honest persons. In case motivation is taken care of, the honest and hard workers are appointed at key positions, not only the work would be performed well but a message among the rest of the staff and the public would be conveyed that the administration is fair, just, positive and responsive.

14. Training: Substantive emphasis must be laid on training of and re-orienting the administrative functionaries. The feeling which has developed among them that they are the masters of all the trades and the theory has nothing to do with the practice is the most dangerous thing. They must be acquainted with new developments taking place in the country and also at the global level and the techniques being made use of for dealing with different facets under different environments must be imparted to them. Behavioural changes need to be brought in their attitude. They must be vigorously sensitised to the significant aspect that they have a particular role to perform for the service of the people. The training culture has to be built up and the training programmes conducted in accordance with their needs of the service.

15. Inspiration: The top leaders in the administration must inspire their subordinates. The juniors must be encouraged, developed, and trusted upon. They must be shown the right path. A corrective attitude coupled with appreciative behaviour should be there instead of a punishing and reprimanding attitude. The seniors must protect their juniors and the bosses should mould themselves as ideals for the subordinates. The seniors should attempt to resist political pressure and should themselves not adhere to any wrong practices. The juniors must be inspired to do rightful acts and encouraged to report cases of unjust pressures being exercised upon them by the political leaders to their superiors so that they could take up the cases with the concerned political authorities.

16. Apolitical Administration: The administrators should not attempt to be committed to specific leaders and political parties. Once the administration becomes political and deviates from neutrality, an impartial and judicious working can not be expected of them. It does not only harm the interest of the system and the citizens but also that of the administrators. One set of administrators having equation with a group of political leaders can seek benefit when that group is in power but should then be ready to face the consequences when the other group comes in power. Thus they earn the wrath of politicians, their administrative colleagues, and, above all, the citizens. The administration has to remain non-political and its being so would help make it more responsive.

The present system with all its evident drawbacks could function better if the administrative actors perform their role adequately. Of course, they are not the only actors but certainly are the ones with a more significant role to play.

B. Political Executives and Leaders

The political leaders also have to work in accordance with some principles and norms as they are more responsible to the people for making the administration responsive. The suggested ways include:

1. Streamlining the System: The political executive has the ultimate authority in a democratic polity. The rules and policies are formulated by them. The political executive must see to it that the policies enacted percolate down in clear and understandable language without having ambiguous, conflicting, contradictory and unexplained legal terms in the same. It would help the administration to implement them smoothly.

Secondly, the political executive should avoid populist politics. They must not announce policies which they are not to formulate in a particular fashion. This would not make the citizens expect from the administration what has not been framed accordingly.

Thirdly, the political leaders, especially the ministers, must own responsibility and should not ask the bureaucracy for putting up the cases in the way which suits the politicians.

Fourthly, the political executive must have a fresh look at the rules and regulations and obsolete and redundant rules must be done away with. For example, a simple rule is that every affidavit must be signed by an Executive Magistrate. Why so? Why can't we trust the citizens, and more so does it mean that in the present system all the affidavits being attested by the Executive Magistrates are true. This type of mistrust rather leads to more wrong things, besides creating a feeling among the citizens that the administration puts the people to inconveniences.

Fifthly, the ministers should look at only those cases which involve crucial decisions. Why the cases like transfer of a Teacher, or creation of the post of an Assistant is to go to the minister. It leads to unnecessary delays whereby the administration's working is affected.

And, sixthly, the political executive must try to reduce the areas of its operations and should encourage more and more NGOs to come on the scene.

2. *Training of Political Leaders:* The profession of politics must be made a respectable one having credibility like that of medicine or teaching. Educated people should enter politics. Political leaders and functionaries must be made to undergo detailed training and orientation programmes and courses so that they are not only sensitised to their own role but also know about the role of administrators, administrative practices and procedures, and the administrative constraints. This would help them to understand things and stop them from putting unnecessary pressures on the administration for wrong things.

3. *Norms and Ethical Code:* It has been viewed by almost all the distinguished persons contacted that there is a substantive change in the overall behaviour or attitude of the political leaders. It is felt that at the lower levels things are worse, but they would remain so unless leaders at the top change their functioning styles. Keeping in view the goals enshrined in the Constitution for getting to the poor of the poorest the maximum for their upliftment, recognised political parties at the Union and State levels must frame a set of norms and a code of ethics for political leaders and functionaries to abide by the same. They must devise a self-denying ordinance so that none behaves in a manner which derails the system or the officials function in an uncalled for manner. Once things straighten up at the highest level, there is no scope for such a thing to happen at the lowest levels. This would help in bringing in the required changes in the system and the political leaders would provide a corrective check on the administration instead of the alleged wrong pressures.

4. *Mechanism for Working Together:* Presently, the administrators blame the political leaders and the leaders blame the officials. The citizens blame both the politicians and the officers. The political leaders in consultation with the administrators must attempt to evolve a workable mechanism in accordance with which the obligations of each are judiciously complied with. Feeling of trust and respect should be developed for each other and all the time each should not be preoccupied with finding fault with the another. This would go a long way in making both the politicians and the administrators responsive to the citizen.

C. Local Institutions

Local elected bodies are in a very bad shape. It also cannot be denied that these institutions can pave the way for a better responsiveness of the administration. For enabling them to do so, the political leaders and administrators are to ensure:

1. *Strengthening of Local Bodies:* The political leadership and the administrators must not feel reluctant in decentralising the powers and authorities and should strengthen the local bodies. These local bodies must not be superseded or dissolved or suspended on whims of state politicians and administrators because of personal, political and administrative reasons. The local bodies must be encouraged and helped to ensure their effective working. The deliberations should be meaningful and the decisions taken by the local representatives must be given weightage by the state politicians and district and state administration. The role which could be performed by these bodies can not undertaken by anybody else in an effective manner.

2. *Effective Leadership:* The local bodies are considered to be the nurseries for democracies. Unfortunately, the promising leaders do not find enough scope at the local levels and do not wish to stay at that level alone. The leadership at the local levels is not up to the mark. The institutions must be given more powers so that talented leaders find scope to work over there and the political parties' organisations at the national and state level should decide to have leaders with more potentials and capabilities in local bodies so that they can contribute their best. Further, local leaders also must desist from pressurising the local administration for wrong acts as it affects adversely the functioning of the administration. The administrative responsiveness could be ensured with more efficacy, in case the strengthened local bodies work effectively and in co-operation with and as a check on the local administration.

D. Voluntary Organisations and NGOs

Voluntary organisations, non-governmental organisations, pressure groups, and consumers' forums, if they work above the petty interests, could bring about substantial improvements in administrative functioning. These organisation should work in the larger interests of the sizeable sections of the society strictly in accordance with their aims, objectives, and goals. Neither these bodies by themselves nor the administration should attempt to dominate the administration. These must remain apolitical. The assistance rendered by these organisations can lessen the burden of the government, an aspect which the government is now seriously examining.

E. Citizens

As mentioned earlier, the total functioning of the government and all its agencies is meant for the benefit, welfare, development, and uplift of the citizens. The system expects some co-operation from the citizens as well so that it could provide them the best of service. The following factors could make citizens co-operate better:

1. Education and Awareness: The citizens must be educated and made aware of the various policies, procedures, rules and regulations and the constraints of the administration. The citizens must be told to co-operate with the administration. The administrative agencies have a major role to play in educating and bringing about awareness among the citizens. Besides, the voluntary organisations, pressure groups, educational institutions, and other social institutions must endeavour to educate the citizens to this effect. But above all, the citizens must develop an urge for understanding various facets and try to have better moral standards. They must not show their impatience and reach the conclusion that the administration is biased and so the way out is only either getting political pressure exerted or adopting corrupt means for getting their work done. They must know that alongwith their rights they have some duties as well. Such attitude of citizens would solve a good number of problems being faced by them as well as by the administration which ultimately would make the administration respond to the citizens needs in a better way.

2. Getting Above from Self: The citizens must feel a sense of pride for being nationals of an independent country. They must realize that everything is not centred around one's own self but the rules, regulations, and procedures in existence are for the overall interest of the society. Citizens must not tend to be possessive about small things at the cost of the state, nation, and society. If the nation would develop, the constituents would naturally develop alongwith it but if a particular individual would develop at the cost of state or society then such personalised development would not last long. Citizens are the only force which could bring about changes in the system if it is corrupt or lethargic. But such a move could be made only by those who are not corrupt and dishonest themselves. All are citizens first and then anything else. Unfortunately, we aspire for what the system could get us. We never think of what we could or should give to the system.

3. *Expectations Within Limits:* Hope sustains life. It is a fact that the citizens of an independent country must have hopes from the government and the system. It is a healthy sign also to say that Indian citizens' expectations have increased. This shows their urge for development. The unfortunate thing is that our expectations have increased much more than what the system is capable of coming up to. This particular factor reveals the selfishness of the aspirants. We have started aspiring for more than deserving the same. The net result is that the citizens keep on pressing and pressurising the administration. Consequently, the administration is neither able to fulfil increased expectations nor provide what the citizens actually deserve. The citizens must appreciate the constraints of the system and cooperate with the administration in regulatory and developmental tasks.

MODEL BUILDING

An analysis of the important aspects relating to the major theme of the present work — administrative responsiveness — has been made in the preceding text. Besides bringing to the fore the meaning, need, and significance of the response of the administration to the desires, wants and genuine expectations of the system, society and citizens, the viewpoints and perceptions of some of the top political leaders and administrators have been referred to and analysed in the light of the major thrust of the work. On the basis of all the variables which are responsible for the prevailing quality and quantity of the responsiveness of the administration, an attempt has been made to present an Administrative Responsiveness Model.

Administrative Responsiveness Model

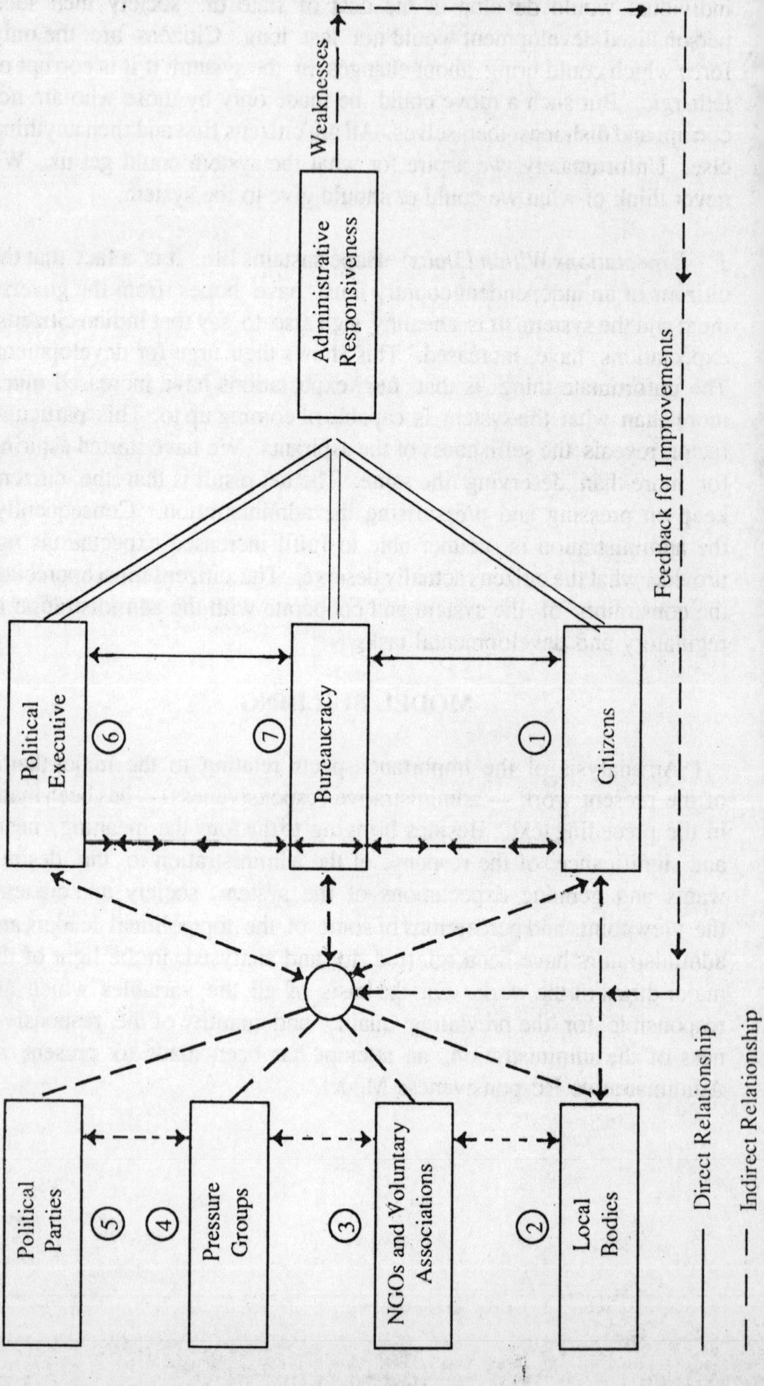

Different forces play their role in improving or decreasing the responsiveness of the model. An analytical examination of the discussions made reveals that there are seven such forces which are interacting with each other and their not doing so in an appropriate manner affects the administrations' response to the public as well as to the system. Though administering is the major function of bureaucracy, other related facets have also an important role to play for ensuring service being rendered to the societal inhabitants in the best manner. There are two types of indications in the model in the form of clear straight lines and dotted lines. A look at the figure reveals that from force number 1 to 7 there are dotted lines which are interacting with the preceding and the succeeding forces. The clear straight lines show a direct interaction between the citizens and the bureaucracy and between the political executive and the bureaucracy. Besides, there are clear both way indications of interaction between the political executive, the bureaucracy, and the citizens. Forces numbering 2,3,4 and 5 in the model, if they operate with a seriousness of purpose, would always facilitate and help the system of administration become more responsible and responsive. Furthermore, it would induce all related facets to be conscientious to their roles and obligations. The result would possibly be the required response of the administrative functionaries and the system which is the need of the day and is unfortunately lacking. There is always a scope for more improvements to be ushered in any accepted system because it is dealing with human beings in the wake of more and more technological advances and developments within the system and at the global level. In order to cope with it, the model has a scope for bringing about the required changes. It is shown as being centered around forces, namely, political executive, bureaucracy, and citizens, with the underlying assumptions that these forces are more predominating and improvements in these would, bring in requisite change and betterment in the performance of the remaining forces because of their being under the influence and impact of the forces numbering 1,6 and 7.

As a result of interaction between different facets, what needs to be done and what would be the resultant of the same, with regard to each and every facet, is mentioned in the following table:

FOCUS	REQUIREMENTS	RESULTANT
CITIZENS	1. Commitment to the society and state	1. Awareness
	2. Understanding of Rules	2. Expectations within limits
	3. Deserve and desire	3. Genuine grievances
	4. Co-operative attitude	4. Approaching Right authority
	5. Logical interests and expectations	5. Care for rules and procedures
	6. Self-denying ordinance	6. Patience and Morality
LOCAL BODIES	1. Appropriate Status	1. Target centred policies
	2. Adequate Finances	2. Cordial relationship with political executive
	3. Meaningful Leadership	3. Owning Responsibility
	4. Sound and effective deliberations	4. Check on administration
	5. Need based policies	5. Facilitating administration
	6. Status-Responsibility	6. Quality Relationship with NGOs and Voluntary Association
NGOs AND VOLUNTARY ASSOCIATIONS	1. Adopting need based projects	1. Adopting neglected areas
	2. Selfless working	2. Lessening Government functioning load
	3. Co-operative functioning	3. Relationship with local bodies and pressure groups
	4. Seeking required help from government	4. Mobilizing Public Support
	5. Debureaucratic Structure	
PRESSURE GROUPS	1. Logical protection of Interests	1. Check on administration
	2. Mobilizing public opinion	2. Facilitating administration

	3. Meaningful suggestions	3. Suggesting required policy alternatives
	4. Ethical working	
POLITICAL PARTIES	1. Interest of society at large	1. Sound Policies
	2. Efforts to streamline	2. Avoidance of Alienation
	3. Asking for required policies	3. Ethical working
	4. Co-operative attitude	4. Check on administration
	5. Thrust on development	5. Facilitating administration
	6. Corrective criticism	
POLITICAL EXECUTIVE	1. Clear and sound policies	1. Effective implementation
	2. Understanding administrative dynamics	2. Non-exertion of undue pressures
	3. Judicious use of discretion	3. Doing away with obsolete rules
	4. Work for all	4. Streamlining structure
	5. Thrust on socio-economic development	5. Keeping administration away from politics
	6. Code of ethics	6. Ethical working
	7. Commitment to Constitution	7. Corrective check on administration
	8. Avoiding populism	
BUREAUCRACY	1. Understanding of role of administrators and politicians	1. Stremlined structure
	2. Effective policy implementation	2. Understanding of policy implementation
	3. Neutrality	3. Supplementary channels promoted
	4. Promoting supplementary channels	4. Promotion than governance
	5. Quick grievances redressal	5. Fixing levels of authority

6. Cohesive working	6. Procedural improvements
7. Seeking co-operation of all	7. Inculcated awareness among citizens and politicians

It has been mentioned in the different sections of the book that the administration in the period immediately after independence was not as bad as it is now. The functionaries used to have some commitment to their obligations as well as to the society in general. But after independence due to one reason or the other deterioration has stepped in the administrative system and the present-day picture is very dismaying. The corruption is at its top, red-tapism, inefficiency and the nepotistic attitude are standing in between the citizens and the administration, the system and the administration, and the society and the administration. Hardly there appears to be any innovativeness in the system of the administration. Because of the government's concern for development, internal compulsions and external environmental pressures are on an increase and would be more. The internal problems are becoming more complex and innumerable challenges are being thrown to the administration. It is expected that the developmental thrusts and challenges would be more and more. The administrative officials and the system of administration shall have to seriously think of building its credibility in the society, and bring new innovative techniques to cope with the tasks so that not only the present problems are solved but also it is prepared to cope with the demands of the future.

Indians used to be subjects having less education, more fear, and little role in electing their representatives in the pre-independence period. Post 1947 era made them citizens, education and awareness increased, and the citizens got the full right of electing their representatives as per their choice. All these factors increased their expectations. It is also a fact that such a tremendous change in the status of the people from subjects to citizens made them expect more than what the system and its functionaries could provide. Unfortunately, even their genuine expectations are not being fulfilled and complied with. The administration shall have to prove its worth by getting their due to the people without their asking for the same. The compliance of the demands and expectations by the administration would speak of its responsiveness to the society at large. The genuine expectations of the people are that the policies which have been formulated must be implemented at the earliest. It is proposed that the implementors must adopt a well-spelt out mechanism whereby the policies are implemented at the earliest. This in itself would go a long way in coming up to the satisfaction of the people. It is strongly felt that in the policy implementation mechanism the implementors must go in the following phases: clear understanding of the policy statement, its goals and objectives; clarity about the target area and groups; prioritising the work to be undertaken; listing the manpower, financial, and infrastructural requirements; asking for more resources, if required; allocation of resources out of the available ones; educating/training the functionaries put on different jobs; educating the public about the policy's benefits and limitation; mobilising public support and forming public opinion through formal and informal channels; and effective monitoring and evaluation.

Effective and prompt execution of various policies would make the public draw a sense of satisfaction with the working of the administration. In case of unjust expectations or the ones which could not be complied with because of one constraint or the other, the administrative agencies must make it abundantly clear to the expectants and should not make any deviations from their stand in the wake of pressures being exerted in some of the cases. Such deviations would reduce the credibility of the administration amongst the majority of those whose expectations have not been met with.

One of the major factors responsible for the increasing gap between the citizens and the administration is the aspect of redressal of grievances. A grievance is any discontent or dissatisfaction with any aspect of the administrative set-up. It can be real or imaginary, legitimate or ridiculous, stated or unvoiced, written or oral. An administrative agency concerned gets a large number of grievances from the people. It is believed that a substantial number of these grievances are either not redressed, or if redressed, it is half-baked, delayed and after causing a lot of harassment to the aggrieved person. It is also a fact that a large number of grievances received are not genuine but vague and flimsy. The question arises: are the genuine ones redressed? if so, with how much efficiency and effectiveness. The administrators could improve their image a lot if they start making use of proper techniques for the redressal of grievances. There could be four such techniques:

a) Monitoring -- By this one means that the head of the organisation should make effective supervision over the areas and functionaries; should have village/ward wise detailed record available with him; should make extensive touring of his area of operation; should have detailed information regarding schemes being executed by his agency; should have vital statistical data readily available with him; and should make periodic inspection of offices/branches under his jurisdiction. Above all, he must ensure that the grievances received are properly kept in record and not only each and every grievance received is acknowledged but also the action taken on the same and the time likely to be taken for the redressal must be communicated to the person concerned.

b) Rules and Regulations -- The functionaries concerned with the redressal of grievances must have detailed knowledge of rules and regulations for taking appropriate action; must attempt to simplify the procedures for the benefit of all; must use discretions but with logic and reasoning; must understand the problems before taking action on it; and as far as possible allow the law to take its own course. No special effort should be made to help one or the other unless the functionary feels satisfied that on a particular logic the case needs to be decided in a specified manner.

c) Seeking Public Co-operation -- The functionaries must be oriented to seek public co-operation. It would help them not only in redressing the grievances but also would reduce the number of grievances. The administrative officials must not hesitate in meeting the public or their representatives; should involve the public in making decisions for evolving implementation mechanism; should immediately act on the grievances, and should evolve a mechanism for eliciting grievances from the citizens.

d) Effective Working -- The procedure for dealing with the redressal of grievances must be laid down clearly. A proper record of receipt of grievance, acknowledgement of the same, whether found genuine or vague, action taken, complainants satisfied or not, if dissatisfied what further action taken, etc., must be up to-date. For all this, besides monitoring and supervision, what is required is: clear instructions, better co-ordination, adequate delegation of power, qualitative decisions, and, above all, fixing of responsibility on the defaulters and appreciation for the earnest workers.

Sound and efficient working of the administration regarding

grievances redressal would not only bring forth the responsiveness of the administration but the techniques mentioned in the mechanism would substantially bring down the quantity of the grievances received by the administration.

The policy formulators frame the policies and the permanent executive implement the same for the peace, development and uplift of the citizens. What is required is the appreciation of roles of not only oneself but that of the others as well. A feeling of trust, dependence, and getting alongwith each other is required. Instead of this there actually is absolute mistrust and suspicion for each other. Everyone feels that his interests are not being protected and the remaining one or two are playing a negative part in the same. The relations between citizens and the administration, between politicians and administrators and between politicians and citizens cannot be improved at the initiative of one particular agency or force. The best of cordiality between citizens and the administration and between the politicians and the administrators could be ensured if both the forces in each equation selflessly and qualitatively contribute to that. Through all concerned quarters, may it be educational institutions, voluntary organisations, pressure groups, political parties, political executive, bureaucracy, and institution of family, this spirit needs to be inculcated amongst all concerned. Lack of understanding between one another would always stand in the way of building a system having responsibility and responsiveness elements.

The politicians feel that the bureaucracy is not performing its role, the bureaucracy has the belief that political functionaries do not let it do its duty appropriately and fairly. The citizens have the impression that both the political leaders and administrators have the least concern for them. All this has created an atmosphere which is to the satisfaction of none. Could the things be allowed to move like this? Why the political executive, major opposition parties, and the administrators don't attempt to bring out a mechanism for working alongwith each other. Why the standards can not be set and made obligatory for all to adhere to. Who stops the ruling/administering forces to find out a way which could work for the development of the nation and the uplift of the citizens. Finding faults with each other and blaming one another would not solve any problem but would rather add to it. If the 'powers and forces' are really interested in sorting out the issues, they must come out with some workable mechanism.

Evolving a workable mechanism would help establishing a code of ethics, set of norms and values which have to be adhered to by all concerned. No exception should be permitted. It is a matter of shame that each person is busy robbing the state and the society. The basic human values are just a thing of the past now. The government is required to stipulate norms. The educational institutions must be instructed to endeavour to inculcate basic human values and national spirit among the children so that they grow up with the same and find the same in practice around them being children as well as being grown up citizens. Nothing short of it could improve upon the system to have responsiveness towards the citizens and society. The techniques and skills referred to could only facilitate the administrative system to work more effectively.

Index